FRENCH COUNTRY LIVING

FRENCH COUNTRY LIVING

CAROLINE CLIFTON-MOGG

photography by Christopher Drake

RYLAND
PETERS
& SMALL

LONDON NEW YORK

SENIOR DESIGNER Sally Powell
SENIOR EDITOR Henrietta Heald
PICTURE RESEARCH Claire Hector
PRODUCTION Patricia Harrington
ART DIRECTOR Gabriella Le Grazie
PUBLISHING DIRECTOR Alison Starling

First published in the USA in 2004 by
Ryland Peters & Small, Inc.
519 Broadway
5th Floor
New York, NY 10012
www.rylandpeters.com

10 9 8 7 6 5 4 3

ISBN-10: 1-84172-602-8
ISBN-13: 978-1-84172-602-1

Printed and bound in China.

Library of Congress Cataloging-in-Publication Data

Clifton-Mogg, Caroline.
  French country living / Caroline Clifton-Mogg ;
photography by Christopher Drake.
    p. cm.
  ISBN 1-84172-602-8
Includes index.
  1. Interior decoration--France. 2. Decoration and
ornament, Rustic--France. 3. Country homes--
France. I. Drake, Christopher, 1950-
II. Title.
  NK2049.A1C57 2004
  747'.0944--dc22
                                        2003022336

contents

introduction

There is an enormous charm in the distinctive decorative style inspired by the French countryside. The romantic landscape, with its small farms, sleepy manor houses, and narrow, medieval village houses, remains a vital part of French life, and the roots of most French people—whether their home is a rural retreat or a chic city apartment—lie firmly in the countryside.

France has been populated continuously for thousands of years, and its natural style is founded on a love and respect for tradition—tradition in arts and crafts, and tradition in a way of life. Modern country style has evolved from these traditions.

In attempting to define something as nebulous as the decorative aspects of French rural style, one realizes that at its heart is not so much a set of rules or dictums, but rather a feeling. A sense of natural comfort and elegance is found in every aspect of French country living—from the manner in which objects are arranged in the rooms to the way in which things are used. There is a lack of clutter, but at the same time an all-encompassing visual feast.

French country style has always influenced interiors across Europe and America. Anyone who has acknowledged a wish for a tranquil environment, a need to be surrounded by natural things, and a liking for soft tones, subdued shades, and natural materials is expressing a debt to the rural style of the French—for what you see on the surface is not the way it is; there is always a further layer, a hidden depth.

The first part of this book, The Elements, looks at the components that make up the whole—the subtle color palette, the traditional materials, the furniture and textiles, as well as the distinctive, often unchanging, objects and accessories, from ceramics to pictures.

The second part, The Spaces, looks at the overall style, the way things are put together in all the main rooms—kitchens and eating areas, living rooms, bedrooms and bathrooms, halls and corridors, as well as that most vital of country spaces, the outdoor room.

If the look inspires you, remember that, for the French, country-style decoration is produced in rather the same way as a perfect meal; each ingredient is chosen with care, valued for its own sake, and then cooked with thought to become a dish that pleases all the senses.

Bon appetit à tous!

the elements

LEFT In this living room, a color palette characteristic of French country style has been used, with soft blues, grays, and whites on walls and furniture. The only hint of pattern to be seen in the room is in the subtle color and designs of the rugs that have been laid on the polished wooden floor.

RIGHT On this upper landing, the pale gray walls are strengthened by the deeper dove gray used in the alcoves and on the panels above the doors. Contrasting with the gray are the plaster moldings in bright, creamy white. The gray-and-white marble tiled floor anchors the rest of the scheme.

color

The French rural color palette is like no other. Even if the technique itself is not always used, the impression given is that the base color has been washed over, creating the effect of a multi-layered film of color over a creamy background.

On first telling, the names of the colors associated with the French country interior sound much like those of colors used anywhere else—blue, gray, cream, green, pink. Simple enough, you might think, but—as always with the French—the difference lies in the way they tell it.

French colors are mixed to a particular subtlety and depth—if that sounds as if they might be boring or dull, nothing could be farther from reality. However, it is true that nothing shouts, and there is nothing about the colors that is either flashy or exhibitionist. These are colors that both soothe and evoke interest, which have character and depth, which are designed to alter in different lights—but also always to complement and enhance the other elements of a room.

The natural light of a particular terrain affects the way in which decorative colors are perceived. France is a large country, and the light changes dramatically from the north to the south (as well as from east to west). These natural differences are reflected in the way colors are used—both inside and out. The farther north you travel, the more you

LEFT One of the tricks of success when decorating a room with a French country palette is to avoid combining sharply contrasting colors. Attempting to create a harmony of complementary tones may be a more challenging endeavor, but the end result will make it all worthwhile.

ABOVE The calm atmosphere in this bedroom is created by the painted wooden walls—finished to look almost as if they had been powdered. A screen, which is used as a freestanding headboard, has been covered in a neutral material, and the unusual polished-concrete floor reflects all the colors back.

find shades that are paler and more limpid, echoing the huge northern skies. In the predominantly sunny south, however, the tones are stronger and more definite—reflecting the sharp contrasts to be seen in the surrounding landscape.

Traditionally, of course, the colors used were dependent on the local pigments. Different areas used local ingredients to make the pigments; other traditional recipes included lime washes and milk washes, and gray- or green-toned distemper.

White—as a decorative color, rather than a no-choice neutral—has always been favored by the French. Their white

LEFT When pattern is added to a traditional country scheme, it is always in the form of a subtle design—in this instance, a fragment of faded 18th-century boiserie hung above the bed.

RIGHT This room was originally the kitchen, hence the pleasing panel of ceramic tiles set into the wall beneath the window. The design echoes in miniature the larger design of tiles on the floor, and every element is kept deliberately low-key.

BELOW Painted wood paneling and two uncluttered pairs of curtains in a classic but striking design are all the decoration that is needed in this simple room with its polished wooden floor and natural rugs.

does not have the cold brilliance of a modern acrylic white, but is instead a subtle, sophisticated oil-based white. It is represented in the white paintwork set off with gilding, as admired by Madame de Pompadour, and the soft whites favored by Marie-Antoinette when she played at country life in the Petit Hameau; such rustic, gentle tones were supposed to reflect the natural, simple quality of Marie-Antoinette's life away from court (although it should be said that that particular queen's idea of simplicity would possibly not have been shared by most of her subjects).

These French whites are sometimes creamy, sometimes touched with gray, and often have the soft, granular texture of white chalk. Very often several different shades of white were and are used together—a look much admired by the late English interior decorator John Fowler, for example, who

As you travel north, you find paler, more limpid shades that echo the huge northern skies; in the mostly sunny south, the stronger, more definite tones reflect the sharp contrasts in the landscape.

was himself much influenced by the French color palette of the past. Fowler would combine many different—but only slightly different—tones of white, some on woodwork, others on plaster details and in panels; he was always looking for a harmonious, restful, architectural composition that suggested rather than dictated.

Other neutrals are also popular in the French country palette, but again they always have a subtle twist. Rather than a clear cream, for example, a soft putty color—cream mixed with an infinitesimal amount of gray—can often be seen. Indeed gray, whether combined with white or not, is pretty ubiquitous; a pale version of gray was the popular color of the 17th and early 18th centuries, often contrasted with off-white—an immensely sophisticated combination. This domestic gray is not the institutionalized, rather dead tone often seen in French municipal buildings, but a more delicate color—almost luminous, lighter, reflective, and often with a pale

ABOVE Although there are several large pieces of furniture in this room, they do not overwhelm the space because the colors have been kept to the traditional palette of blue and gray tones, with white fabric on the bed and at the windows.

RIGHT This 19th-century house has been sympathetically restored. In a simple child's bedroom, the period fireplace takes center stage; everything else, both in color and design, is subservient to its mass.

LEFT The colors in this comfortable living room are neither bold nor intimidating. The cupboard is a fine antique *buffet à deux corps* (one cupboard above another), colored in soft pinks and grays. The two antique armchairs—known as *chaises à la reine*, and dating from the reign of Louis XV—are left polished and pale.

pink or blue base that gives it a fresh or warm tone. And the color is often mixed or contrasted with other shades of gray—a chalk gray might be teamed with a deeper, dove-wing gray in panels and woodwork, for example, and lifted by touches of creamy white.

From gray comes blue and—except in those interiors that are influenced by the hot climate of the Mediterranean—most French blues are reflective, reflecting colors, used to calm and soothe. When gray-blue is not the chosen color, a commonly seen alternative is a watery, pale turquoise, often again used in combination with creamy white.

As with blue, so with green. In nearly all French greens, whether they are pale or strong, there is a little gray—or sometimes black—in the background. Not for France the cheerful emeralds or mown-grass greens favoured in other countries. Subtlety is the goal, and the prize.

ABOVE A circular stone basin, echoed by a handmade circular window framed in iron, gives a unique character to a corridor. These essential elements are left to stand on their own, with the surrounding color in the simplest of shades.

RIGHT AND OPPOSITE In these two bedrooms, the texture of the walls becomes the color and the pattern. Made from a mixture of mud and hay, the walls represent a relatively modern version of traditional techniques such as the Native American adobe finish—and it would be a shame to paint or decorate them further. In the larger of the rooms, the floor tiles—made to a traditional design of terra cotta bordered with oak infills—have been reversed to show the original terra-cotta finish.

ABOVE The walls in this alcoved bedroom have been finished in a pale turquoise, almost duck's-egg blue; the stucco decoration has deliberately been left unrestored, giving the impression that it might be trompe l'oeil rather than real. Beyond the alcove, soft gray has been used with a deeper color on the woodwork. The highly polished terra-cotta-tiled floor sets it all off.

ABOVE RIGHT In this corridor leading into the brick-floored room where winter logs are stored, all the wooden surfaces have been painted slightly different shades of blue to give a subtle effect.

OPPOSITE, LEFT French country bedrooms in the rural style—often notable for their lack of decoration and accessories—give particular prominence to textiles and color. In this room, a fine antique mirror is the sole decorative piece, with the result that the viewer's attention is focused both on it and the room's subtle colors.

OPPOSITE, RIGHT The ubiquitous washstand—part of the essential furnishings of a French bedroom—stands under and supports a grand, rather ornate mirror, which is also painted, rather than being gilded in the traditional manner.

From gray also come mauve and lilac—either as bright as the color of violets or or closer to the quiet, almost musty tones that are quintessentially French, and which look so winning when teamed with gray-green, perhaps used on woodwork. A more sophisticated combination that is sometimes seen is a gray mauve offset by a dark, almost terra-cotta red—the red known as sang-de-boeuf makes a particularly effective contrast.

Pinks and peaches are also to be found among the range of French country colors, but they are not childlike nursery tones—there is nothing of a sugary or sweet nature about them. Like so many French country colors, the pinks and peaches appear almost organic, seeming as though they might have emerged from the color of the original plaster rather than having been applied on top of it and, again, they often seem to include a hint of pale gray ancestry.

No country color palette could be complete without yellow, but French yellows stand apart from their competitors in tone and warmth. The yellows that French people prefer to use in their interiors are on the whole neither too sharp or strident nor too deep; they are the yellows that are easy to live with and acceptable to all—diluted chrome yellow, saffron mixed with white, and butter yellow softened, appropriately, with cream.

Then there are the decorative color combinations—those important marriages of woodwork and wall. It is rare in France—at any rate, among exponents of this particular style— to observe a strong, violent, or dramatic contrast in a room. A subtle combination, something that pleases or interests and which incorporates other elements of the room, is preferred. The French have never felt that the only color for woodwork is white—in fact, in many cases, they consciously shy away

from this most obvious of tones. If white is used, it will be an off-white, but it is just as likely to be gray; it may be green or blue, or even a mixture of the two.

In a French country house, all the interior elements that are fabricated from wood—not just the architectural frames— may be coated in paint. Like the Scandinavians, the French particularly like painted furniture, and the soft and subtle colors they favor are as effective on furniture as they are on walls; to the French, a painted finish is as charming, if not more so, than the patina of old wood.

Dedicated paint strippers take note: in the 17th, 18th, and 19th centuries, furniture was, as often as not, painted—and those who today religiously strip back any painted pine piece they find in the name of authenticity are destroying its charm by changing it into something it was never intended to be.

Nowhere in true French country style can the link between the past and the present be more clearly seen than in the choice of materials utilized both inside and outside the home.

The emphasis on natural materials means that the combination of textures chosen is very important. When everything stems from the same natural core, harmony is attainable—indeed, pretty difficult not to attain. Floors are basically bare, which allows the material of the floor—whether it be stone, terra cotta, or wood—to provide the interest; floor rugs range from the simplest of plaited or woven grasses to decorative antique rugs whose old beauty is flattered by the simplicity of the floor.

WOOD

A wide variety of woods is evident in rural interiors, but the woods used in different parts of France were and are largely those from the trees growing in the surrounding countryside—fruit woods such as walnut and cherry, and traditional hardwoods such as oak and elm. Exotics such as mahogany or maple will not be found in abundance here, for self-sufficiency is the name of the game.

In true French country style, wood is ubiquitous and the most popular material, both inside and

materials

The materials typical of French country style seem to come from the landscape itself, from the surrounding countryside, where natural life predominates. Wood, stone, terra cotta, and metal—these are materials as old as the land itself and have been continuously used since dwellings were first constructed there.

LEFT AND RIGHT In a seamless integration between the interior and exterior, the floor of this hall is covered with the same loose pebbles from a river bed that are to be found outside. The half-plastered walls reveal the original stonework inside the alcove, and the simple wooden bench is designed to blend into the natural background. The steps that rise up to the house beyond are treated in equally simple manner, the only contrast being the internal wooden shutter, made simply in two panels.

out. Outside, as well as the obvious doors and windows, in almost every region of the country, exterior wooden shutters are used, not just for their practical qualities, but also—and this is characteristically French—as what can only be called a design statement: carefully painted in a color that is often unexpectedly strong and that contrasts boldly with the more traditional façade.

Inside, baseboards and framing are wooden, and wooden-framed furniture—indelibly associated with French taste—is seen everywhere. Much built-in furniture is also made of wood, again sometimes stained or polished, but usually colored in a sympathetic tone. Sturdy wooden beams—more often than

not exposed—are sometimes left in their natural state, but are more commonly painted or color stained; it is all part of French country style.

No discussion of French interiors could pass without mention of wood paneling; paneling, whether painted or polished, is one of the greatest decorating devices known. It can correct faults in a room, add gravitas where none existed, and give emphasis in the subtlest of ways. Why do we always associate wooden panelling with French interior decoration? After all, other countries use panels, wood or plaster, in their decorative schemes, but there is something indelibly French about the idea of paneling, even when it is actually trompe l'oeil.

From walnut and cherry to oak and elm, the woods used in the rural interior are those found in the surrounding countryside.

Of course, wooden floors are laid throughout France, both in the country and in town, and since French country style eschews wall-to-wall carpets, the finish of any wooden floor is highly significant. It might be wood-stained, sealed and polished, waxed, pickled, or colored—either with a painted finish or a tinted stain. The look is natural, the color rarely strong, for the important element is that the wood remains, on balance, natural.

STONE

Very often in France, indeed as often as possible, stone is used as a floor paving inside the house. The thought of this may bring a shiver to any of us who live under northern skies, but stone is not in fact as cold as it is painted (or should that be polished?).

The joy and beauty of stone lies in being able to appreciate its variations and range of tones, which comes about when it has been cut or chiseled in a sympathetic manner. Although new stone takes time to weather well, old stone—and it does not have to be very old—has a softness and variety that is immensely appealing.

Hand-cut stone is obviously preferable to the machine-made version, and indeed there are few examples of the latter to be seen in the French countryside. When paving stones are old, subdued, warm, and glimmering, there is little to trump them.

ABOVE AND OPPOSITE **This bedroom is a good illustration of how to mix natural materials to achieve a look that is remarkably comfortable and welcoming. The simplicity of the basic elements— the heavy wooden beams, the drystone wall behind the bed, the polished wooden floor—might be a little austere on their own. But the addition of specific furnishing elements—a bed that invites sleep and relaxation, the heavy white curtains that combine warmth with luxury, the comfortable armchair and stool, in addition to the well-placed lighting—transform the whole enviroment. These pieces, coupled with the neutral palette and the textural differences, all convey a soothing and very comfortable atmosphere.**

LEFT When a wall made from local stone is constructed in this almost organic way, in steps that resemble a terraced hillside, the result, far from being harsh, is soft and full of charm.

BELOW Natural materials look best when combined with other, similar textures. Here, a simple wooden buffet, a chair made from wicker, logs in the fireplace and a bucket filled with dried flowers add up to a nature feast.

RIGHT In this bedroom, the severity of the stone walls is softened by the comfortable bed with its plump pillows and decorative appliqué quilt. The room incorporates a bathroom—the bathtub is hidden behind a half-wall beyond the bed.

Although most stone lovers are happy with carefully cut rectangular slabs, for aficionados of decorative stone, the most satisfactory use of the material is on the floor in the form of cobbles—inside rather than outside the home—where the rounded shape of each stone brings texture as well as a sculptural quality to a room.

TERRA COTTA

Since clay is found throughout France, terra cotta—particularly in the form of tiles—has become ubiquitous in French interiors. Although it is strictly speaking a manmade rather than an entirely natural material, terra cotta has acquired credibility from its long history—the fact that it has been made for thousands of years, and used both inside and outside. The Romans are traditionally credited with being the first to have produced it.

Both terra cotta and its close companion, brick, are characterized by a sensuous warmth that come from both the color and the tactile presence of the

Unplastered stone walls, perhaps not seen as frequently today
as they once were, may sometimes—if properly treated—seem
to shimmer with a shadowy softness that can be most appealing.

LEFT, ABOVE AND RIGHT Wherever possible, exponents of French country style like their floors to be made from natural materials—not for them the joys of easy-clean synthetics. Terra-cotta and brick tiles are always prized. There is a warmth and a depth to these, and years—maybe centuries—of use mean that each one has an unique texture and color. The fact that they were made individually gives them a pleasing irregularity as well a distinctive tone and color. There are several different traditional shapes—each of them charming, and most of them in use since the Romans first made them; most commonly found are squares, brick-sized rectangles, and narrow paver types.

materials; even terra-cotta tiles that have been finished with a modern sealant have a friendly, comforting feeling—a sense of elemental earth—which is, after all, what the material intrinsically is.

Terra-cotta floor tiles come in several traditional shapes—not only large and small squares, but also long, thin, paver-style rectangles and hexagonal shapes. They can be glazed, and smaller-version glazed terra-cotta tiles are often used for wall and surface tiles as well as for covering floors; the glazes often appear artlessly simple—just a hint of the

original clay appearing beneath a patchy washed surface—but, like so much in the French country style, the final effect is carefully thought out and achieved only with skill and taste.

METAL

Would it be an exaggeration to say that a house that has been designed or evolved in the French country style could hardly be in the running were there not metal incorporated somewhere in the scheme? A little strong, perhaps, but there has long

Like brick, terra cotta has a sensuous warmth that derives both from its color and from its tactile presence. The Romans are credited with having been the first to produce the material.

LEFT In this welcoming kitchen, the floor tiles, laid in a traditional diamond design, are from le pays de Bray in Normandy— new terra-cotta tiles made in the old way. The wall tiles are old, but not originally from this house; interestingly, they are the same tiles as those found on the walls of the Paris Métro.

RIGHT Antique tiles such as these old Delft tiles are widely collected today and are frequently seen in country-style kitchens. They can either be used on their own or mixed with modern tiles, made into a pleasing, irregular design. Alternatively, they can, as here, simply be kept on display to enjoy and admire.

BELOW These heavy floor tiles have been brought to this house from farther north—Noron la Poterie, near Bayeux. Their dark glaze contrasts with the pale upholstery of the chair and the simple cream-colored curtains. The decorative urns have been imported from Spain, where they were used to store oil and olives.

been in France an affinity with metal that is not necessarily shared by other nations. Traditionally it was the *ferronier* whose art and skill wrought and cast the iron into sympathetic and beautiful shapes—and the material is just as popular today in and around the house as it was 300 years ago.

Quite apart from its use in making occasional furniture—think of those little round outdoor tables and twisted chairs so beloved of cartoonists—metal is used in the windows and on the stairs. There are bowed and bulbous window grilles, sinuous stair rails and banisters, as well as kitchen fixtures and door hardware. Somehow the craftsmen seem to be able to forge and turn the material into designs which, although complex, are also light and airy with, sometimes, an almost rococo feel.

CONCRETE

A relatively new material that is now widely seen in the French country interior is concrete, sometimes plastered or polished, sometimes left in its pristine glory. Used to make built-in furniture—perhaps a seat or a storage unit, or in the kitchen a sturdy sink unit, concrete can be colored and textured to work with the rest of the room.

LEFT In a house built in the late 19th century, this traditional country chair is very much at home. Although simple in design, with its rush seat and painted frame, there is an elegance about it which would not be out of place in a far more elaborate setting.

RIGHT A traditional white-painted buffet is used as a display hutch. Country artefacts such as decoy ducks and a birdcage combine with large glass bowls and a pair of tall lamps to make a decorative group, reflected in a wood-framed mirror, painted in the same tones.

furniture

French country furniture is extremely well adapted to its function, and each piece is polished or painted to show off its lines to best effect. Traditional, natural materials are always used, and the pieces themselves seem strangely organic—as if they are growing up from the earth in rounded, comfortable shapes.

The characteristic pieces of furniture found in a French country house, whether the dwelling is large or small, combine immense charm with intense practicality. Traditionally, it was the obvious practical solution to use local woods to make local furniture, and that remains the case. In northern and central France, light-toned fruit woods such as cherry and walnut are found, as well as occasionally (and more often in the south) olive or mulberry wood.

But although French country furniture is based on the natural materials at hand, and is designed to play its part in the country house, it would be wrong to describe it as rustic—a word that can often imply a twee, almost painful, self-consciousness. A better word would be rural, which could be defined as simple in style and designed for a specific purpose. Think of the benches, tables, straight-backed hutches, and armoires that can be found in almost every French country home; they look as though they belong and are happy to be in place. That is in fact the case, since the story of furniture design throughout history is the story of adaptation: pieces originally commissioned for the rich and fashionable were, over time, adapted and simplified for use in less exalted households. From seating to storage,

Although they are nothing if not practical and supremely well adapted to their particular function, pieces of French country furniture are also immensely decorative and easy to live with.

LEFT Iron is a common feature of French country style, and here it has been shaped into a very simple but fine-lined, curved-arm day bed. Plump cushions—some of them white to harmonize with the curtains—give it a comfortable air, and sisal matting covers the floor.

BELOW This enticing antique bed with its wooden head and foot board could only be French. The cane insets are traditional, as are the painted frame and the white linen. No rug adorns the polished wooden floor.

from the buffet to the armoire, designs and styles emerged that have stood the test of time and are still made today. But they are not clumsy: there is, in country pieces as well as in city pieces, a delicacy about French furniture that is often lacking in its English equivalent—a certain subtlety of line that is unique, and which has something to do with the materials used as well as the lightness of touch within the design.

The style has become famous; there are one or two almost iconic designs that can be found throughout rural (and not so rural) France, which are just as sought after today as they ever were. Take perhaps the most instantly recognizable piece in any French household: the armoire—the large wooden storage cupboard that could, and can, be used in any room. Upstairs, an armoire is usually used for linen and clothing, and in the kitchen for storing kitchenware or food—although when used as

OPPOSITE A traditional chair looks just as much at home in a bathroom as in other rooms. Here the chair is combined with the plainest of wooden tables, a pair of striking striped curtains, and another decorative birdcage—all on an old terra-cotta-tiled floor. Each element is simple, but the whole makes a charming group.

LEFT The imposing all-purpose armoire in this bedroom has been put use as a clothes closet. The size of the piece—painted, in the traditional manner—means that the room needs little additional furniture other than a wooden table and rush-seated chair.

RIGHT In this old kitchen, with its charming floor of hexagonal terra-cotta tiles, a grand old 19th-century armoire has had its door panels glazed, rather than being left open or backed with chicken wire. The cupboard is home to everything from bottled preserves to large plant pots, vases, and other essential dishes.

BELOW Doors removed from an old armoire have been recycled in this dining room to hide a large number of bookshelves.

a *garde à manger*, or larder, it often appears in the form of a lower cupboard with doors surmounted by open shelves, perhaps protected by a grill made of chicken wire.

This useful object—a cupboard combined with open shelves—can be found today in any room in the French country house: in the living room holding books and objects, in the kitchen as a holder of dishes and cooking equipment, in the bedroom with linen and other bits, and in halls and on landings as general repositories of belongings.

Such cupboards are sometimes whitewashed, and often painted or color-stained. The inside

ABOVE An ornamental dresser dating from the 18th century has been both decorated and painted in a fairly intricate fashion. Its decorative appearance means that it is most effectively displayed as here—on a plain wooden floor, and flanked merely by a pair of branched sconces.

ABOVE RIGHT This graceful bedroom dresser, taller than is often seen, is designed in curved serpentine form, with a marble top to match—a typically French country combination. Painted blue and finished with decorative ironwork, it works well with the upholstered armchair beside it.

OPPOSITE, LEFT On this very simple, painted Louis XV cupboard is hung a picture dating from the end of the 18th century. The picture rests against an antique panel that still retains its original paintwork. On each side of the cupboard stand a pair of faux marble columns, also dating from the end of the 18th century.

OPPOSITE, RIGHT In a large and airy bedroom, complete with an iron four-poster bed, is a fine 18th-century Swedish *buffet à deux corps*. Made in serpentine style, the piece dominates the room, complemented by a floor of hexagonal terra-cotta tiles.

surfaces might be painted, or lined with traditional patterned paper or fabric. There is also a small *garde à manger*, still often seen, which looks more like a wooden, wire-fronted cage and was customarily hung from the ceiling or high on the wall to keep the contents out of sight of hungry people.

The buffet, or low cupboard, is another popular piece of furniture which was traditionally used for both storage and display. Frequently designed with serpentine curves, the buffet sometimes has an upper tier that might be simply shelves, or might be another, smaller cupboard, when it is known as a *buffet à deux corps*. Like its more capacious relation, the armoire, it can be of polished or painted wood, and otherwise decorated or adorned with carving or paintings.

Up until the 17th century, in most countries, chairs were still straight-backed, formal objects, designed to reflect the

status and position of the sitter and to command respect rather than to offer comfort. But, in France, something was afoot. A new type of seat was in the process of being invented—something that made sitting a pleasure, rather than a duty; indeed, it would not be inaccurate to say that the French invented the armchair.

From France came the comfortable, low-backed, feather-stuffed armchair; the *bergère*, a tub chair with upholstered arms and cushions; the *marquise*, a love seat; the *canapé*, an intimate sofa; and the chaise longue, on which hours could be spent enjoying the latest fashionable novels—all designed for relaxation and enjoyment.

Although now overtaken by the ubiquitous upholstered sofa, the rush-seated banquette is still sometimes seen today, and much sought after in its antique incarnation. Known in France as a *radassié*, this type of banquette looks like an extended wooden-backed arm chair and convivially seats three or four.

The French country-style bed is many things, but what it is not is a divan with a upholstered base that extends to the floor. It may be constructed from metal or wood, but it will be free-standing, and it will almost always have both a head and a foot, perhaps finished in a distinctive decorative style. This has always been the case. Traditionally, beds were symbolic as well as utilitarian pieces—often highly decorated and ornamented. Although not loaded with quite so much symbolism today, the bed still represents one of the largest and most important pieces of furniture in the house and therefore is often decorated and—if it has posts—hung and draped accordingly.

A lesser piece, but one which is instantly recognizable as belonging to the French country style is the marble-topped

During the 17th century the French invented the armchair, an inviting seat that transformed sitting from a duty to a pleasure.

ABOVE LEFT The traditional French sofa, or settee, more closely resembles a benchlike banquette than the over-stuffed, sprung piece that passes for a couch elsewhere. Refinements to the basic shape include upholstering the back and seat. In this example, the ties wound around each leg add a contemporary touch.

ABOVE In this version of a *chaise à la reine*— a design virtually invented by the French—the upholstered frame and matching squab cushion make for an irresistibly comfortable seat.

LEFT It is relatively unusual to see a piece of furniture in a French country-style house upholstered in anything other than a plain, neutral fabric. If a pattern is used, it is virtually always a stripe or check—both of which, as shown in this example, work very well with the clean lines of the formal chairs.

OPPOSITE Although it has found a home in a French house, this magnificent 18th-century armoire comes not from France, but from northern Italy. The main difference between it and its French counterparts is evident: the ornamentation and the paintwork are far more elaborate, with decorated panels and cornice.

BELOW **A striking piece of kitchen furniture has been fashioned from a simple buffet with an unusual set of shelves above it—two tiers connected by finely turned supports.**

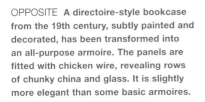

OPPOSITE **A directoire-style bookcase from the 19th century, subtly painted and decorated, has been transformed into an all-purpose armoire. The panels are fitted with chicken wire, revealing rows of chunky china and glass. It is slightly more elegant than some basic armoires.**

ABOVE **No piece of furniture or element of decoration in this kitchen has been allowed to create a distraction from the overall atmosphere of calm. Everything has been painted the same bleached-gray tones. The only note of color can be found in the tiled floor.**

washstand to be found not only in bathrooms and kitchens, but also in halls or on landings—anywhere where a basin or sink may be installed. These are nothing if not sleek updates from the past; where once the basin would have been a portable bowl in a set with a pitcher, now it is an inset polished bowl, complete with faucets.

The photographs in this book make it clear that there are very few pieces that look as if they have just landed haphazardly in a room; even more than in a highly sophisticated, urban interior, the furniture in a French country house has to be chosen—each piece with care—because each piece matters very much. Yet what doesn't matter is whether it is new or old or a combination of both—it is the look and the purpose that counts. There has never been in French country style a barrier between old and new. Perhaps that is because, although the furniture may be rural in concept, there is a undoubted sophistication to it—an innate delicacy and subtlety of line that is unique to the French, and which manifests itself in the materials used as well as in the lightness of touch applied to color and finish. French country furniture is immediately recognizable; although it is nothing if not practical and supremely adapted to its particular function, it is also immensely decorative and easy to live with.

LEFT Everyone loves vintage textiles—particularly in the French countryside. Boutis, the traditional quilts, are widely collected and used throughout the house. In this instance, several boutis have been stored in another traditional staple: the scrolled wire or metal basket.

RIGHT A bed with an 18th-century headboard has been finely dressed with old textiles. The folded bouti is a Louis XV textile known as an "indienne"—an early chintz that was particularly fashionable in the 18th century. Underneath it is a 19th-century cover made from the underskirt of a lady's petticoat; when the fashion changed, these underskirts were frequently made into bedspreads. The pillow covers are also of indienne type but are decorated in new designs based on traditional patterns.

fabrics

Traditional textile designs and patterns are far from scorned by lovers of French country style: still produced today, they may sometimes be recolored or brightened up, but the designs that were first made widely available during the 18th and 19th centuries are still just as popular as they ever were.

French rural interiors are dominated, albeit subtly, by fabrics. Textile designs and colors, and the inventive use of fabrics throughout the home, are a vital part of the entire look. In every room, textiles appear in profusion—not just as curtains and blinds, but on chairs, over benches, as cushions, and on beds and tables. As expressions of both color and design, fabrics lift every other element in the room.

It is fascinating that textiles designs created in the 18th and 19th centuries are appreciated as much in modern times—both in the cities and the country—as when they were first taken from the blocks. It is a testament to the brilliance of these early designs that today—whether recolored or newly reproduced in the original color combinations—they can still blend in with, and often enhance, modern design and decorative schemes.

Designs range from small, precise, geometrically governed patterns to stripes of every size and color. There are romantic florals—sometimes vastly oversized and reminiscent of an overgrown garden—and vast scenic prints such as the familiar designs associated with toiles de Jouy.

Toiles de Jouy are as irrevocably associated with French interiors as croissants are with a French breakfast. Even among those people who do not

Textiles are seen in profusion—as curtains, blinds, and cushions, on chairs, over benches, on beds and tables. As expressions of color and design, they lift every other element in the room.

immediately recognize the name of Jouy, there can be no mistaking the designs. In the middle of the 18th century, Christophe-Philippe Oberkampf started a manufactory using copper plates to print cottons at Jouy-en-Jousas, a village on the road between Paris and Versailles. The popular taste for printed designs on cotton had already been determined with the importation a century earlier, through the French East India Company, of calico and chintz—known as "indiennes," after their land of origin. So popular were these new textiles throughout France that they were seen as a threat to the Lyons silk-weaving industry, and a ban—which was in place for 50 years—was imposed on the manufacture or sale of all printed cottons both imported and produced at home. As soon as the ban was lifted, Oberkampf was one of the first to take advantage of the new freedom, and in 1760 opened his works, employing Christophe Huet, one of the great designers of his time, to create exciting new designs for the receptive buying public.

The factory was soon enjoying huge success; the new copperplates for printing were far larger than earlier models, which meant that the designs could be far wider in scale—up to a square yard

OPPOSITE **Even the smallest piece of antique textile can inspire decorative ideas if you use lateral thinking. In this bedroom, an old scalloped valance, presumably one of a pair, has been used to beautify a pair of very simple, very long curtains. Although the fabric gives the room a lift, it is not strong enough to overwhelm the rest of the simple scheme.**

ABOVE **Three different designs have been incorporated in this small area—an approach which, decoratively speaking, is rarely recommended. Yet because they have been carefully chosen—and even though the cushions are in a toile design and the window seat and chair are in coordinating stripes and checks—the final effect is pleasing to the eye.**

ABOVE, FAR LEFT Striking contemporary pillows have been made using a subtle combination of 19th-century linens. Each one is inset with a central panel consisting of an embroidered monogram from antique linen sheets that once formed part of a trousseau.

ABOVE, CENTER LEFT This late 18th-century, Louis XVI provençal chair has its original rush seat. Overstuffed cushions in traditional designs make it as inviting as it was 200 years ago.

ABOVE, CENTER RIGHT A collection of old textiles—here stored in the ubiquitous armoire—can be made to look attractive even when they are not in use or on display. In this instance, the different designs have been stacked according to color and pattern, creating an interesting and decorative design.

ABOVE By being stretched, hung, and displayed across an old wooden door, an antique wall hanging introduces a surprising and innovative decorative touch to what would otherwise have been a plain corner.

BELOW, FAR LEFT Although attractive, this ornate forged-iron bench from the 19th century might be a trifle uncomfortable; it has been made inviting by the addition of a row of pillows. Scraps of 19th-century linens are used to cover both the pillows and the seat.

BELOW, CENTER LEFT Different patterns and designs can work successfully together as long as there is an underlying theme. In this case, it is color—although no two designs are the same, all have blue as the dominant tone.

BELOW, LEFT Elegant antique country chairs should be upholstered in designs and colors that do not overwhelm; here, pale traditional checks in soft pink add to, rather than detract from, the lines of these beautiful chairs.

in area—and Huet capitalized on this by creating designs that ranged from chinoiserie fantasies to antique follies, pastoral scenes, and even military triumphs. Napoleon was a great admirer of Jouy designs, and several of his military campaigns were immortalized as printed cottons—as well as other popular events and games and sports of the day.

In one sense, those famous toiles sum up French textiles: appearing at first sight almost artlessly simple, with their limited palette and monochromatic combinations, with designs that are recognizable at quite a distance, these toiles are actually deeply sophisticated. In the best examples, the colorations are

incredibly subtle. The blue is not just any blue—it is an inky, gray-touched blue; the red is madder with other tones in it; the violet is again tinted with other shades; and the brown is as soft as 19th-century drawing ink.

The indiennes that were produced by the enterprising Oberkampf in the 18th century, which feature motifs based on traditional Indian and Eastern designs—including the adaptable and ever-popular Tree of Life design—also remain very popular today, with many designs combining geometric and floral motifs. In addition, it is still possible to find literally hundreds of variations of small regular flower designs—the sort of pattern

that is often associated just with the South of France, but which actually occurs throughout France, and which comes from a peasant tradition of motif and design.

Although stripes are international and timeless, there are two stripes that seem more representative of France than any others. The first is traditional mattress ticking; this was originally confined to blue and gray, but is now available in several modern variations. The second is not actually one stripe; rather, it is a design incorporating several stripes of different widths, and frequently comes in subtle color combinations of blue, buff, old pink, and creams. Both variations are much used to cover

OPPOSITE, LEFT **Simplicity always triumphs over complexity in the French country style. The simple design of these curtains works well with the flower-printed wallpaper; hooked simply onto rings, they need no lining since external shutters diffuse the light.**

OPPOSITE, RIGHT **What could be more charming than plain, simply headed white curtains tied back with narrow lengths of printed toile, caught as high as a child's sash? Nothing else is necessary to complete the look.**

ABOVE LEFT **Country textiles all share an affinity of design and of color; stored in a pile when not in use, these quilted covers and traditional eiderdowns look as pretty as they are comfortable.**

ABOVE **Variations on a theme: an antique iron day bed has been dressed in a winning mixture of a fragile, soft blue print on the seat and, for the cushions, a stronger, reworked ticking design in deep blue and white. The diamond-shaped floor tiles become part of the overall design.**

Toiles de Jouy are as irrevocably associated with French interiors as croissants are with a French breakfast. Even among people unfamiliar with the name, there can be no mistaking the designs.

ABOVE **As the colors that are generally used for soft furnishings are never overwhelming or loud, they tend to work together without too much trouble; in this room, a chinoiserie toile design is used for pillows, paired with very pale ticking stripes in the same soft pinkish-brown tones.**

RIGHT **Another reason for the compatibility between different patterns and designs is that strong color contrasts are rare. On this Louis XV day bed there are two quilts—one antique, the other new, as well as pillows in different fabrics, including some made in an 18th-century toile de Beautiran.**

fitted or squab seat cushions throughout the house, as well as in blinds and simple curtains.

What is important is that, whether old or new, all these textiles are, in French country style, always used with restraint. At the window, elaborately made and designed curtains with swags and tails are rarely seen; more usual are unadorned curtains hung from metal poles, although they are often embellished with unusual brackets and finials. Sometimes a scalloped or straight-edged valance is hung across the top of a window frame—particularly effective when it is a piece of antique toile de Jouy.

Boutis are enthusiastically used both on beds (for which they were originally designed), as throws and covers on sofas and chairs, and as dress cloths for tables. Boutis were traditionally bedspreads or quilts—made, as their counterparts in America and Britain were, as warm decorative coverings for beds, and often embellished with accomplished and elaborate stitching. The antique version of boutis are avidly collected today, but new ones, in the same soft color combinations, can also be found and look very effective, especially when several are used in combination.

Antique textiles themselves are much collected in France. Brocante fairs—a cross between junk and antique sales—are held throughout France on a daily basis, and there are many antiques stores that

THIS PAGE **This bedroom under the eaves, with its sloping ceiling and exposed beams, has a bed with a carved wooden headboard painted in traditional gray, and a quilted, flowered boutis. The curtains are tied back with toile de Jouy in the same soft tones of pink.**

ABOVE **The pillows on the bed have been covered to match the quilt, and there is a subtle contrast with the checked and striped linen beneath.**

RIGHT **Full-length lightweight curtains need balance; here it is provided by a deep hem at floor level and an even deeper valance, which breaks up the height and adds decorative interest.**

specialize in textiles of all types. Many of these are based in Isle-sur-la-Sorgue, a town in Provence that is a country antiques lovers' paradise.

Antique textiles generally are much in evidence in French country interiors. For many devotees, no piece is too small or too insignificant to be used somewhere. Not only is toile de Jouy collected, but other, less-known toiles, such as toile de Beautiran and toile de Rouen, are also sought after. All of these textiles can be made into cushions, of course—both scatter cushions and neat, tailored squab cushions used on rush- or cane-seated chairs—and pieces that are too small even for

a cushion might be used as central panels in a larger piece. Textile pieces are used draped over beds, sometimes over a boutis, as well as to cover headboards, and they are also seen as runners on buffets and chests.

Old linen sheets—which are still relatively easy to find, although becoming rarer—are much prized, too, particularly those that are monogrammed and embroidered. They still serve as sheets, but also as bed covers. They may also be used as tablecloths or as starched, unlined, lightweight curtains; even when a sheet is damaged, a decorative use can still be found for it—it can be cut up and used to cover cushions.

LEFT It is always worth moving familiar objects into a new setting in order to see them anew: these antique hanging lanterns, of simplest design, have been placed on a wooden shelf against a stone wall and flanked by bunches of drying lavender. Their simple shape can be better appreciated against the rough background.

RIGHT In an old bastide, and in a room dominated by a rough stone wall, a striking arrangement has been created using simple urns and jars. Grouped together, they form part of a larger composition involving a pair of candelabra and other decorative objects. More delicate objects would have had no impact in this robust setting.

accessories

Every object used to decorate and adorn French country interiors was first made with another function in mind—another life, in fact. Few things of beauty are discarded in the French country home; when an item loses its usefulness, it can still be admired as a decorative object, particularly if it has acquired some of the patina that comes from years of use.

Those objects that are loosely known as accessories —the decorative wherewithals that give a house its individuality and character—are alive and well in the French country house, but they are accessories with a difference. In keeping with the ethos behind the style of the French country house, there are few pieces to be seen that have been selected for their decorative value alone—which is not to say that they lack elegance. There is an elegance, of course—why wouldn't there be?—but it is the elegance of use, rather than the elegance of ornamentation.

Ceramics, glass, metalware—much of which certainly has acquired a patina of age—are to be seen everywhere in the French country home. The pieces of ceramic and glass look neither fragile nor mean of spirit; cups and glasses are easy to grasp in the hand, plates stack into satisfying piles. First and foremost, they have definite shapes—shapes to enjoy using as well as looking at.

Rather fittingly, considering French people's preoccupation with cooking and eating, anything and everything connected with the kitchen is used as added decoration—from glass storage jars grouped to make a chunky composition or china jugs filled with garden flowers to baskets stacked one inside the other in a heap. In one room there may be a group of assorted pitchers and drinking glasses; in another, earthenware cooking pots of

ABOVE, FAR LEFT **Against a background of antique and new tiles, an antique relief-molded pitcher is used as a decorative container for a few carved-handled knives and spoons.**

ABOVE, CENTER LEFT **Old flatware appreciated for its shape is kept in a worn and well-used kitchen table drawer.**

ABOVE, CENTER RIGHT **Against an unbleached linen cloth on a painted iron table is a set of old plates printed with a design of blackberries and their leaves.**

ABOVE **All household linen once had stitched marks, varying from the embroidered monogram to the simple, traditional cross-stitched initials seen here.**

BELOW, FAR LEFT **The blue and white traditionally printed china harmonizes with the white serving dishes and tureen as well as with the soft blue-gray painted chairs.**

BELOW, CENTER LEFT **An armoire has been used to store a collection of Provençal earthenware in many different glazes; the beautiful pieces are in everyday use.**

LEFT **As these silver- and bone-handled knives show, knives and forks can be as finely designed as china or glass.**

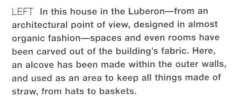

LEFT **In this house in the Luberon—from an architectural point of view, designed in almost organic fashion—spaces and even rooms have been carved out of the building's fabric. Here, an alcove has been made within the outer walls, and used as an area to keep all things made of straw, from hats to baskets.**

ABOVE AND RIGHT **Shelves have been put up to store earthenware, glass, and pots in this kitchen and eating area built into the extension.**

different sizes and shapes, or metalwork baskets filled with eggs or fruit. Collections of decorated coffee and tea pots are grouped on chest tops, and large and small candlesticks are used on mantelpieces and tables. It is simply a question of imagination—and of looking at familiar objects in a different, more lateral light.

Glass is enthusiastically collected everywhere in the world, but in France it is seen predominantly as an expression of the pleasures of the table, rather than something to be hidden away in closed cabinets. Wine glasses and other glasses are often stored outside the kitchen cupboards, on windowsills or tables, where their lines and design can be admired; carafes and decanters, too, are often grouped together in a pleasant composition, ready to be pressed into use.

Glazed earthenware cooking dishes and pots may be handed down from generation to generation and are highly prized. In the French countryside they are not banished to the kitchen, but are used throughout the house, with the most decorative examples being displayed with pride on bureaux and buffets.

Pitchers, the all-purpose containers, are used in every room, not simply for holding liquid. Filled with flowers or just grouped on shelves and tables according to color or shape, they are the answer to instant decorating French country style—all jugs and carafes are generous and flowing of line, often quirky in design, and automatically convey a strong decorative presence.

Large urns and jars of stoneware or glass—the sort of container traditionally used to store olive oil—are particularly popular in French country decorating. Simple and striking, they are put on the floor, underneath tables, in a corner by a staircase or door, for example, or placed on top of cupboards and bookcases, both to give height to a piece and to add depth to the room. They are also much in demand on the terrace or in the yard.

Although there is much fine porcelain made in France—think of the ornate wonders of Sèvres china—in the country, stoneware and tin-glazed earthenware, known as faïence, are more easily obtainable and, to many people, preferable. They also work far better decoratively in a country interior than more delicate pieces. Different regions of France produce their own variations of faïence, but generally they can be found with deep-colored glazes—typically intense mustard yellow, dark rich green or soft creamy white through which the basic clay can be seen.

Hand-painted faïence, from centers like Moustiers, and creamware—earthenware with a cream body, first made in the 18th century to imitate porcelain—is also widely collected, and can often be seen in country rooms, piled up or displayed individually.

Even cooking pots and pans are used to make a decorative statement—particularly when they are of well-buffed copper. Bowls, saucepans, colanders, and skillets are hung, either on the wall or from the hooks of a ceiling-suspended rack. Other metalware includes the twisted and woven baskets sometimes used for storing eggs—and even, in one house, old wire whisks, collected together and hung on a board above the kitchen sink; the different shapes and sizes of the twirling whisks make a pleasing and witty composition.

Although pictures can be seen on some of the walls in these homes, they tend not to be hung in quantity nor grouped closely together in a geometric composition. That is French city style—in the country, such matters are treated more subtly, with

one large picture, or perhaps a pair, hung in close conjunction with a piece of furniture or other objects. It will be seen as part of a group, and there will be a meaning in its position.

Mirrors, on the other hand, are not so subtle. They are used with flamboyance in every room: gilded mirrors, oversized mirrors, mirrors like suns, mirrors like garlands; they are everywhere, reflecting light from outside back into the rooms.

No thoughts about the style of decoration in the French countryside would be complete without mention of the most accessible and attractive accessory of all: plants and flowers. Every room has something green and living somewhere—from a basil plant in a pot in the kitchen to mixed bunches of garden flowers or cut branches of flowering shrubs. In buckets and goblets, pitchers and tubs, usually artfully unarranged, flowers set the true French country tone, and complete the connection between garden and house.

LEFT These elaborate sconces, draped with necklaces of crystal, have been hung, in traditional fashion, on each side of a mirror, where their color tones have been chosen to echo and complement the gesso-based gilded mirror frame.

OPPOSITE Traditionally, lighting is an area of interior decoration where style and function easily combine, and nowhere more so than in the traditional chandelier shape. This metal example, hung on a long chain at the top of a stairwell, is Italian and dates from the 18th century.

ABOVE A joy of glass-hung chandeliers is that colored crystal or glass can be used to give a new dimension to the decorative qualities of the lamp itself. Different colored drops—often available separately—can always be combined into a piece of charm, as in this pretty sconce.

LEFT The more a chandelier resembles a beautiful necklace, the more it appeals to the senses; this one, with its looped garlands and drops, is perfectly placed in a room decorated with a traditional flowered-column paper and set off with an oval ancestral portrait.

Mirrors are used with flamboyance in every room: gilded mirrors, oversized mirrors, mirrors like suns, mirrors like garlands; they are everywhere, reflecting light from outside back into the rooms.

THIS PAGE **The enormous mirror has been given a starring role from an unusual perspective. Placed on the floor between two windows, the ornately framed looking glass reflects the bed and the arresting decorative piece—a cross between a wheatsheaf and a sunburst—that hangs above the bed.**

OPPOSITE **Decorative features in this grand bedroom come from the architecture, with the deep-green painted and gilded door and the panel above the fireplace painted a contrasting terra-cotta shade. The room's only decorative accessory is a line of chunky candles.**

the spaces

You could say that the French are defined by food—the growing, the making, the eating of it. For it is a fact that locality and specialty are everything in France: local shops sell local produce and so, too—at least as far as fresh produce is concerned—do outlying supermarkets.

As for specialties of a village or region, there is an enormous, well-placed pride in such products. For French people and foodies of other nationalities, certain names immediately, and instinctively, evoke particular foods. Bourg-en-Bresse is renowned throughout Europe for its flavorsome chickens. It is said that the best butter is from Normandy (although other regions of the country might quibble over that), the most scented and fullest melons and cherries are from Cavaillon near Avignon, and the tenderest, sweetest beef from Charolais cattle.

Local food is tied to the concept of seasonality, which is paramount; even in supermarkets, there is a preference for foods that happen to be in season in France rather than those that have been flown in from the other side of the world. And there is no

OPPOSITE AND ABOVE **In this Ile de Ré kitchen, there is a positive mixture of old and new: the tiles are old, but have been brought into the kitchen from elsewhere on the island, and new elements such as the range have been integrated sympathetically into the original fabric. In one corner of the kitchen (above), a charming group has been made by combining pattern, in the form of 19th-century tiles, shape—antique drinking glasses and vase—and color, represented by the ceramic olive jar set against the blue of the tiles.**

kitchens & eating areas

The French attitude to food is profoundly different from that of the Americans or the British. Put bluntly, food for the French is important—really important. Indeed, food probably figures more strongly in the lives of most French people than almost anything else.

ABOVE **A French country kitchen has no need of any ornament that has only a decorative purpose. Each element, including the most ephemeral—a string of dried herbs, for example— is decoration enough.**

ABOVE RIGHT **An old, very solid, wooden chopping block has been put together with a simple antique buffet to make a piece of furniture that is both functional and unusual. New and old combine easily in a proper working kitchen.**

OPPOSITE, LEFT **Industrial design enthusiasts will like this use of the functional as ornament. The shapes of kitchen tools are varied and many, and this collection of wooden and metal whisks is pleasingly displayed on a wooden panel.**

OPPOSITE, RIGHT **All the everyday objects in this kitchen are compatible, and the colors and textures around them also work. The range, the terra-cotta floor, the wooden elements—all go to make a unified space.**

need for farmers' markets in France—every weekly market in every country town is a farmers' market, with stands manned, or womanned, by the farmer or his wife. Drive through France, whether by superhighway or poplar-lined minor roads, and your journey will be periodically punctuated by placards and posters enthusiastically announcing the proximity of some famous, not-to-be-missed specialty of the region—from oysters to apples, from patés to pastries.

This deep and abiding interest—obsession even—with food and eating, means that the French country kitchen, more often than not, really is the very heart of the home. Whether large or small—and usually it is as large as it can be made—it is the command module of the whole house, where everything starts. Preparation, cooking, and eating—all the delights of a satisfying meal—take place there.

The essence of such a kitchen is its equipment. The French country kitchen frequently contains much that has been handed down, and these treasured objects are arranged and displayed with a view to their aesthetic possibilities as well as to their accessibility. This is not to say that there is nothing modern in the French country kitchen—cooks everywhere love a shiny new saucepan—but in addition to the new pieces there will be the pestle and mortar that belonged to a grandmother, or the well-used cutting boards and worn knives that have been handed down through the family.

Utensils and dishes are often stored in the ubiquitous armoire —the large wooden cupboard, originally used for storing linen, which seems to be present in nearly every French country house in one guise or another, with its glazed or chicken-wire-covered doors that allow the contents to be kept on view.

Utensils and dishes are usually in natural materials. The pestle and mortar will be made of wood or stone, the oven dishes of terra cotta or stoneware, the mixing bowls of earthenware, and the chopping boards of wood. The idea is that function is beauty, and because all the implements are made of natural materials, they harmonize and blend in a way that manmade materials do not. There is not so much interest in, and reliance on, contemporary design and up-to-date styling, because the style is inherent in the object.

Although the unfitted kitchen—a room in which not every unit is uniform and not every surface matches—has been heralded over the last few years as a new concept in many places, in the kitchen of the French country house the idea never really went away—you would be hard pressed to find wall upon wall of stainless-steel units and Formica countertops in the average

THIS PAGE AND OPPOSITE **In an old chateau such as this, all the cooking essentials have been stored and arranged to make the most of their natural advantages. A part of the original scullery has been used to house a large collection of Provençal pottery as well as old linen and other items. There is a certain artlessness in the arrangement, which depends more on the quality of the objects to be stored than on the methods of displaying them.**

The French country kitchen contains much that has been handed down, and treasured objects are arranged and displayed with a view to their aesthetic qualities as well as to their accessibility.

ABOVE AND ABOVE RIGHT **The kitchen and eating area in this former Normandy farmhouse combines several different functions, and care has been taken not to remove entirely the link between work and leisure. Originally, the kitchen was home to five cows, and throughout the space old and new are** **used together with relative abandon; the practical yet beautiful kitchen equipment is displayed with pleasure.**

OPPOSITE **The hard-working part of this rural kitchen combines seamlessly with the area where the delights of the country table can be fully appreciated.**

French country house. The concept of the built-in kitchen is not one that sits easily with the French country style, and there is precious little built-in furniture there to be found, unless a line of wooden shelving can be so construed. New and old rub shoulders, and useful adaptation is the key phrase.

Dishes and utensils that are not stored in the armoire might be housed in a buffet—a low sideboard—or even in a chest-of-drawers commandeered into kitchen service, and indeed the

country kitchen quite often contains other pieces of furniture that were not specifically designed to be there, but which are either pretty or useful, or both.

A large central table is often at the center of the equation—both literally and figuratively. It is where food is prepared and also—most importantly—where it is eaten. The sight of the food, uncooked as well as cooked, is important in a French country kitchen, and a table in the kitchen affords the constant

OPPOSITE **A French country home can be of several different periods —additions and extensions being an essential, almost organic part of the architectural whole. In the eating area of this house, there is nothing unnecessary—the central table, surrounded by traditional chairs, is just right for the setting.**

ABOVE **This white-painted version of a traditional *buffet à deux corps* has a simple charm. It also is very functional, displaying china and glass in the glazed cupboard, and fruit on the hutch top, as well as housing the more practical but less decorative essentials within the capacious lower cupboard.**

ABOVE **This old country house, originally a manor house, was built partly in the 17th century and still retains many original features. The fireplace dates from that period, and—as simple as could be—it has been easily incorporated into the kitchen and eating areas, and simply ornamented with functional stoneware pots, tin jugs, and glassware.**

pleasure of anticipation as well as gratification. The table itself is generally made of scrubbed deal or pine, or it may sometimes have a marble top above a wooden base.

Traditionally, dining rooms were not particularly common in the French country house, and although some exist today, it is more usual to see a part of the kitchen devoted to the pleasures of the table. This may mean that the table used for preparing food in the kitchen plays a dual role, or that there is a separate table devoted to dining. Chairs, which will be

positioned where needed, will usually be traditional in style, frequently with rush or cane seats and ladderbacks, and they may all match one another—but there again, they may not.

The sink (or sinks) in a French country kitchen is usually made of stone or ceramic, like a British butler's sink; it is rarely of stainless steel or a synthetic material. The sink unit—if you can dignify it with that name—is usually set into a wooden surface; beneath it are cupboards or, more usually, open shelves, sometimes curtained off to hide the plumbing, and

RIGHT **Strange as it may sometimes seem, the design of the early 20th century is a hundred years away from the present day. In this country dining room, the table dates from the early 1900s and the cupboard doors, bought from one of the many antiques dealers in Isle-sur-la-Sorgue, date from about the middle of that century.**

ABOVE **In this house full of early 20th-century architectural and decorative features, the kitchen sink is about as basic as it could be. Made of stone, with a faucet that seems to have grown out of the wall, it stretches a comfortable distance across the room over open storage shelves.**

RIGHT **Nothing is discarded or put away in a French country kitchen simply because it is not of contemporary or novelty design. This distinctive glassware from the nearby Biot factory has been made in the same way for almost 50 years. It is as charming—and as popular—now as ever it was.**

on which utensils and dishes are stored. It is the epitome of non-design; indeed, the non-design of many of the kitchens in the French countryside can make them appear almost organic, with shelves and other basic storage areas seemingly carved out of the walls and ranged around the room where needed.

Like every other element in this room, the flooring in a French country kitchen is rarely synthetic. Traditionally a tiled floor was laid, and this is still the case today when a new one is required.

Sometimes the tiles are ceramic, but more commonly they are terra cotta, sealed or otherwise, and made in square, rectangular or hexagonal shapes. The days are long gone when the only good tile was an old tile. Now, if a seamlessly traditional look is needed, there are many modern styles of terra cotta that look neither too new nor too old.

Decoration is essentially an affair of the heart, and nowhere is the heart more engaged in France than in the kitchen. The

LEFT This charming room was once a laundry room. The two-part stable door and the white-painted wooden beams are offset by the warm tiled floor, the starched tablecloth, and cushions on the ladderback chairs. Very much of its type, the decorative element—apart from the naïve oil painting—consists of functional objects displayed in ornamental fashion.

RIGHT There is an air of elegant mystery about this room, with its fabric-covered chairs and pristine tablecloth. The abundance of textiles contrasts with the plain wood-paneled walls, simple metal chandelier, and dramatic black-and-white-tiled floor.

colors chosen for the walls will not usually be very strong—there are so many other things happening in the room that bright colors would be a distraction. The shades most often seen are the well-loved tones of cream, off-white, or a little blue or beige.

The textiles, too, will be useful as well as pretty; they will not be dramatic or attention-seeking. There may be small floral patterns or striped ticking cushions on the chairs, and checks or stripes at the windows—although curtains do not play a significant role in these rooms.

What usually adds the color in a country kitchen are the objects and the food itself. There will be the rich tones of French pottery—deep saffron, brilliant green, creamy white, as well as perhaps some traditional painted and decorated pieces from Quimper in the north and other centers of pottery such as Moustiers in the south. There will be woven baskets, and metal work, sometimes polished copper and brass, but above all there will be vegetables, fruit, and herbs; bread and wine. And that, of course, is the point.

living rooms

The contemporary living room has to perform many roles. Sometimes it works and sometimes it doesn't, but one of the success stories is the French country living room—the way in which it fulfills so many different roles in an understated and elegant way, to make a space for living that is also an integral, important part of the whole house.

In earlier periods of history, different rooms had their own separate functions to perform—even the smallest house had a parlor or front room where formal entertaining took place, while ordinary family life was carried on in a cozier room elsewhere. Now, in most homes, one room has to be so many things all at once—somewhere to sit, somewhere to receive guests, somewhere to be quiet, and often somewhere to make a noise.

One of the reasons why the French country living room encompasses with ease so many functions and domestic pleasures is because the French—who, historically, were always ahead of the game as far as interior decoration and design were concerned—really invented the concept of comfort and of passing the time pleasurably.

Prior to the invention in France in the 18th century of the comfortable upholstered chair, there really was no such thing as relaxed comfort in most countries. Upright discomfort was closer to the mark, a combination of utility on the one hand and status on the other—difficult bed mates at the best of times. But in France it was different; by the time of Louis XV, a strict distinction was being made

An iconic living-room piece is the wooden armoire: the often carved, usually tall, and indisputably French cupboard either of solid wood or with open panels that reveal the display shelves.

between those rectilinear, formal chairs that formed part of the architectural fabric of the room—*sièges meublants*—and the new *sièges courants*—chairs designed to be portable. The many innovative styles included the *fauteuil en cabriolet*—a light armchair that could be moved around and which was of fluid shape as well as position. These chairs were carried across to where they were needed—to a table for a game of cards perhaps or into a circle to join in a conversation.

The concept of the comfortable room had arrived, and in larger houses, whenever formality was required, one could always repair to the *grand salon*, a room that remained for some time to be decorated in the traditional formal manner, specifically for those grand occasions.

So it is not surprising that modern French country living rooms are about as comfortable as one could imagine—not only comfortable, but frequently very cozy, and rarely grand or formal, but with a simplicity and understated chic that distinguishes them from similar rooms in other countries.

Informal, of course, does not and should not mean studiously contemporary. Pieces of furniture are always carefully chosen in the French country sitting room, and antiques—as long as they are comfortable ones—are an integral part of the plan, either on their own or combined with a selection of new pieces, which themselves are often designed in traditional manner.

There are certain furniture "givens" in French country house style which, no matter what part of the country you happen

OPPOSITE **An imposing Louis XIV bookcase sets the tone for this country living room—grand with fine furniture but comfortable as well, its inviting sofa piled with scatter cushions. The contents of the bookcase itself are beautifully** arranged, with interesting pieces on every shelf, including pictures, pots, and candlesticks.

ABOVE LEFT **The pier mirror that adorns the wall between these two windows is late 18th century, from** the reign of Louis XVI. Unusually, it has been inset into a carved and gilded boiserie. The console underneath the mirror is Italian and dates from the mid-18th century. The simple curtains serve to frame this pleasing composition.

ABOVE **This high-backed sofa is upholstered simply, to show off the pillows, all of which are covered in 19th-century toiles. The early 18th-century wooden doors have been painted a soothing blue-gray to tone with the rest of the room.**

RIGHT Another aspect of the same living room shows a larger built-in corner seat on the other side of the fire, piled high with pillows. The warm terra-cotta floor tiles mean that the otherwise gray-and-white color scheme does not make the room too chilly.

ABOVE In designer Anna Bonde's sunny living room in the Luberon, all is pale and calm. The sofas are covered in Linum fabrics with pillows of French ticking. A pair of wing chairs make up the group. Anna's drawings add a further dimension to this restful room.

RIGHT Every element in this most muted of rooms is conducive to relaxation. The cupboard doors, complete with their original carved and painted decoration, came from an old armoire. The squashy sofa is complemented by a corner seat built in next to the fire.

to be in, you will see time and time again—and, more often than not, they will be found happily at home in the living room.

First, there is the upholstered sofa, often with scrolled arms, and quite often covered in a neutral material. There will usually be only one, rather than the more urban pair, and there will never be matching chairs. Three-piece sets would not be at home in this particular style—indeed, are they at home anywhere any more? This solo couch may have draped over it what we might called a throw, but which traditionally in France

might either be a boutis, or country quilt, or perhaps a pretty piece of fabric, either folded like a panel or used almost to cover the upholstered frame.

Pillows, too, are used in great profusion on these couches— not intricately designed and sewn ones, but consciously simple shapes, frequently made from just a single piece of old or new fabric, or perhaps a slightly more complex design incorporating a piece of old embroidery or print. More often than not, there will be a design among the pillow covers based on one of

OPPOSITE **This French country house dates from the 19th century—a fact confirmed by the larger-than-usual windows, with their unusual shallow-arched top. The room differs from so many French country living rooms in that is altogether more spacious, with higher ceilings and a notable absence of painted or carved wood.**

LEFT **The imposing fireplace is not, as it might seem, an antique transplanted from the 18th century, but one that was probably made in the early 20th. The simple, 18th-century-style drawing-room chair in pale pink stripes looks perfectly at home against it.**

ABOVE **Sunlight streams through the window, illuminating the modern sofas and classical armchairs. The color palette has deliberately been kept pale and soft, with boutis, throws, and cushions adding color and texture to a neutral background.**

LEFT **The room has deliberately been furnished with care and edited down. There is just enough seating for comfort, and the curtains at the magnificent window have been kept quite plain, attached at ceiling level to maximize the amount of light available. Even the objects on the console table show a high level of restraint.**

the many members of the "indienne" family of patterns, or else a design associated with, or based on, a toile de Jouy.

The next, almost iconic, piece often found in the living room—as well as in almost every other room in the house—is the unfailingly useful wooden armoire: the often carved, usually tall, and indisputably French cupboard either made of solid wood or with open panels that reveal the display shelves. This cupboard may be in polished or stained wood, but it is just as likely to have been painted with soft water-based paints and in equally soft neutral tones, and in it may be found books, objects—anything that needs to be easily at hand. Should the armoire be full, there will often also be a painted, open wooden bookcase to accommodate the overflow.

Where there are occasional chairs, one may be a comfortable English-style upholstered chair and at least one other may be

an elegant, classical French wide-seated chaise à la reine, with upholstered back and cushioned seat and padded wooden arms. This might be old or new, covered in a striped or solid material, and with its wooden legs either painted or polished. A day bed or chaise longue might advance into the room from one corner, and there will also be at least one table at which one can sit, surrounded by straight-backed chairs, possibly with cane seats.

All these pieces are set off by a floor that is as natural as the furniture—the perfect background for the relaxed comfort of the room. It may be wood old or new—boards perhaps, polished and sealed, or sometimes, if the house is old enough, with fine old parquet; or it may be made of terra-cotta tiles or even of flagstones. It might have rugs patterned or plain, old or new, it may even be completely covered—but only with sisal, coir,

Country living rooms are about as comfortable as one could imagine—not only comfortable, but often very cozy, and rarely grand or formal, but with a simplicity and understated chic.

LEFT In this converted bastide, care has been taken to retain both the atmosphere and many of the architectural elements that give the house its flavor. In the living room a massive armoire, put into use as a bookcase, holds its own against the wall of rough stone and a heavy-beamed ceiling.

RIGHT If you happen to have an 18th-century fireplace in your living room, make sure that everything else complements such a definite statement. The buckets of foliage and the flamboyant chandelier give as good as they get.

BELOW Anna Bonde's living room opens onto a small courtyard. A day bed or bench that she herself designed sits across from a chair by the 19th-century maker Thonet.

or another natural covering; wall-to-wall Wilton carpet would not fit the bill. Above all, it will be easy to maintain and renew.

As far as the color is concerned, the interesting thing about the color scheme of these rooms is how little there is of it. In some rooms, the walls and woodwork are dominated by neutrals such as cream, off-white, and palest gray; in others, the colors of the country emerge: corn yellow, wood green, spring-sky blue. What connects all the colors, however many or few there are, is the lack of strong contrast between them and the landscape beyond; there is no more than a blending together of the natural and the imposed.

A domestically important room like the living room must be designed and decorated with an eye to the basic architecture of the building, and scale and balance must be taken into account. These imponderables are all-important in every living

room, and perhaps more so in these rooms with relatively few pieces of furniture. Large pieces make a room work more successfully, and in a country living room it is important that the sofa be large enough to balance cupboards and bookcases—for all would fail if the impression were of overcrowding. Compared to other rooms of comparative size, less is definitely more in the living room; but that is not the point—what has been brought together is really the wherewithal for life.

Perhaps the major difference between the country living room and the city drawing room is the way in which the country room draws on its relationship with the garden or landscape beyond the windows. Ideally, the French country living room will open directly onto the garden or landscape beyond, and everything inside will be directed to that connection.

However small the room is, if it is decorated with care, it will appear to be both light and spacious; the pale tones of all the colors and textures will enhance the reflective qualities of the room, and the lack of strong contrasts will have the same effect. The windows will be curtained in such a way as to emphasize the view through the window rather than the style of the curtain; simple hangings in subtle designs will be used, with little elaboration.

Whether deliberately or not, the French country living room is designed to work with, rather than against, its surroundings—there is no clash of cultures or, indeed, of styles.

Informal does not mean studiously modern. Furniture is always carefully chosen in the country living room and antiques—as long as they are comfortable ones—are an integral part of the plan.

LEFT AND RIGHT A quintessential French rural bedroom is dominated by a comfortable bed with plenty of pillows and cushions; two old painted cupboards and an empty wooden picture frame are both decorative, and—in the case of the cupboards, at least—functional, too. An interesting way to use fragments of antique textiles is to make them into individual pillows that can be used either singly or in groups on chairs or sofas, or on a bed (as shown), where they add a warm touch to an otherwise simply dressed piece of furniture.

bedrooms

A country bedroom should have the same features wherever it is, for the style is universal, tempered by individual and national differences. The style of a bedroom is as much a state of mind as a decorative scheme, and a country bedroom should feel open and airy, with a sense of space and a lightness of touch.

A country bedroom should always be characterized by simplicity. While in some cultures, simple might mean almost austere, a French country bedroom is anything but austere. Don't make the mistake of equating simple with uncomfortable. Simple, in terms of French country style, should mean simply warm, simply pretty, simply comfortable—and simply wonderful—regardless of whether the room is large or small.

French people's regard for comfort and pleasure—as at the table—is far too well developed for them even to contemplate the idea of a bedroom that is not a pleasure to be in. Each element is considered separately, and then all are combined together into a harmonious whole.

Naturally the most important piece in the bedroom is the bed. It is also the largest piece, and should be treated with a gentle hand so that it does not take over and overwhelm the rest of the room. The French country bed is likely to be a bedstead of metal or wood. It may be completely plain or embellished with head and foot boards, or it may be in the form of a simple four-poster. It is rarely a stuffy and stuffed divan, upholstered to the ground.

If the headboard is integral, it might be lightly carved—in the same way that the armoire and buffet traditionally were—but it is unlikely to be of dark-stained and polished wood. Rather, it would be of

OPPOSITE In a master bedroom, a simply dressed bed is made dramatic by the decorative treatment of the walls, where the color to the level of the bed is finished with a yellow wash, while a terra-cotta band beneath ties the wall to the tiled floor.

LEFT The bed and windows are draped with soft, falling white; the chair is covered to match. In fact, the only place in this room not dominated by texture and fabric is the tiled floor, which is in warm, polished contrast to the rest.

BELOW If you are fortunate enough to have such a decorative headboard—this example is carved, painted, and decorated— then little else is needed in the way of ornamentation.

wood that had been pickled or painted—pale and interesting, rather than dark and brooding. Many headboards consist of wooden frames around a cane or textile inset. Styles that you simply would not expect to see in a French country bedroom include ornate, heavy carvings and heavily padded versions, perhaps covered in dark damask or brocade.

Often the headboard is an ornamental addition, freestanding or attached to the wall rather than to the bed. The variations are endless—it could be a piece of old paneling, or a fragment of ornamental plasterwork; it might be an old boutis, a wall hanging, or another material—perhaps a piece of old toile or old linen, used as a hanging or made into a loose slipcover and eased over an existing board. It could be an interesting piece of framed old wall paper, or even a favorite picture.

RIGHT **This bedroom in the Luberon seems to be part of the structure and architecture, with its heavy beams and strong stone wall. In order to sustain the mood, the bathroom has been built out of sight but in reach, tucked behind the half-wall.**

BELOW **Built cozily into an alcove, this bed has been finished with curtains, which hang from a simple piece of molded wood. Checks, stripes, and flowers work together because they are all in similar shades of pink.**

OPPOSITE **Delicate antique furniture makes this bedroom. A Swedish chest dating from the 18th century is placed beside a 19th-century wrought-iron bed. Above the chest, an ornate mirror adds weight to the scheme.**

Many French country beds have hangings—some swing from simple coronas attached to the wall, while others are draped from posts. In the latter case, the hangings are always conspicuously light, both in weight and in design; they are commonly made from voile or unlined linen, and the canopy—if it exists at all—can be as straightforward as a valance around the framework or a piece of material stretched across the frame.

What goes on the bed is almost as important as what decorates it. The bed linen—and it is frequently real linen—may be new or it may be old; antique dealers do a brisk trade in old embroidered and monogrammed linen sheets. It is usually white, although blue—as everywhere in the French countryside—is sometimes allowed to intrude, albeit in a tasteful way; a thin stripe or two of blue perhaps, but certainly not a flower-bedecked field.

Comforters are not as popular in France as in some other countries; sheets and blankets, often covered with a quilt, are more usual. There may be an assortment of pillow sizes – square ones—and probably a bolster underneath. In many instances, the pillowcases will consist of several different designs, all of which will work together, and there may also be extra cushions, again in assorted designs and patterns, scattered across the bed.

The bed cover itself is invariably some form of quilt—either a single piece of material that has been quilted or a patchwork quilt. New machine-made boutis are now widely available, the designs often taken from a traditional indienne or toile design.

Storage for clothes and linen will rarely, in a French country house, be in custom-built systems or closets; it is far more likely that the trusty all-weather country friend, the armoire, will be brought up into the bedroom. In keeping with the lighter, more feminine aspect of this particular room, the armoire will probably be of painted rather than polished wood, and the central panels may be filled with pleated or ruched fabric, adding to the softer face it presents.

Any window treatments found in a French country bedroom are designed to be simple—generally speaking, the French do not set as much store as the inhabitants of many other countries on heavy curtains that have been lined and interlined.

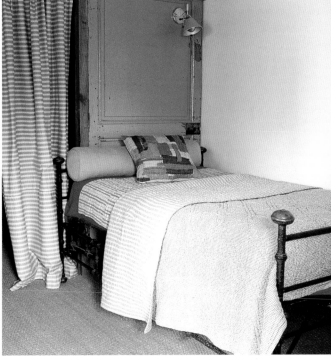

Shutters are to be found throughout the country, both on the outside and inside of the house, and are widely used. Perhaps it is for this reason that French country style demands curtains of the subtlest kind in the bedroom, made from natural-looking textiles and often unlined.

Curtain materials are predominantly voile, unbleached linen, fine cotton in white and pale, cool shades, and the curtains themselves are usually a generous and billowing floor-grazing length. Occasionally, curtains are caught or tied back with a piece of contrasting material or fine cord, but French country style holds no truck with elaborate swags and tails, nor ornate headings of any kind.

OPPOSITE, LEFT **Inside this simply draped four-poster bed, an old French headboard is hung slightly above the bed so it can be seen in all its glory.**

OPPOSITE, RIGHT **In this beamed-ceiling room, the bed is hung with antique sheets used as curtains. They are slotted onto metal rods attached to the ceiling by a central trapeze.**

ABOVE LEFT **A corona without a crown tops this bed, which has been given both a simple headboard and its own antique bust of Eleanor of Acquitaine in an alcove above the bed.**

ABOVE **A beautiful antique boutis—found at one of the many antique shops in Isle-sur-la-Sorgue—makes up for the lack of drapery on this simple iron bed.**

This sounds as if French people do not appreciate bedroom textiles, but actually they do genuinely appreciate them—on the walls. Traditionally, the French country bedroom was hung with material from ceiling to floor, with curtains and bed hangings in the same design. Although this completely cocooned look is not so popular now, many a country bedroom is still hung with material in a toile or flower design, or even a fine-checked or striped cotton. There is a depth and a subtlety to a room finished in this way that is hard to beat.

The bedroom is also probably the only room—in the French country sense—where wallpaper is seen as an acceptable option. Romantics—and where better to be romantic?—are captivated by subtle flower designs, often intertwined with

ABOVE **A color immediately associated with French country style is warm rose madder, one of the dyes used in the printing of traditional toiles. Made into a generous bedcover, the toile is complemented by the checked rug.**

LEFT **A bedroom furnished with two beds is given added privacy by hanging a heavy curtain between the two. All else is light and bright, with lightweight curtains at the window and pale, gentle colors.**

RIGHT **In this room the bed has been simply dressed with a bedspread in deep pink checks, over a dust ruffle of deeper stripes: what could be simpler—or more inviting? Scatter cushions covered in old French ticking complete the look.**

LEFT AND BELOW **On the Ile-de Re, an old domaine has been decorated in classic French country style. This cool bedroom is in a small square tower, and the heavy beams rise into the roof space; the angled tower walls are covered with tongue-and-groove planks that have been painted blue. Although the room is small, every comfort is at hand. The bed itself has been kept simple to maximize the space, with the addition of two sets of blue and white bed linen.**

ABOVE **A charming French colonial iron bed, dating from the 19th century, has been hung simply with gauzy white curtains, tied to the metal frame. This allows the head and foot of the bed to be seen and appreciated.**

stripes in color combinations that are gentle and easy to live with—such as sage green combined with old mauve, or dusty pink and milky gray.

However, of all the decorative alternatives, the most popular —and simplest of all—is the paint option. Painted plaster is the preferred choice for most French bedroom buffs, and the colors follow the palette in the rest of the house: greiges, beiges, creams, and off-whites, but also soft grays, yellows

and dusty pinks with occasionally—in celebration of the bedroom's individual and personal charm—the sort of blue that features so strongly in rococo paintings.

The bedroom floor might be plain, sealed wooden boards or polished parquet, or it might be cool terra-cotta tiles. Rugs are not always a necessity, but if they are wanted, they will be flat weaves or natural sea grass or sisal, in keeping with the calm and easy air of the rest of the room.

LEFT A roll-top cast-iron bathtub and simple white-painted wooden floor enhance the character of this country bathroom. Note the all-purpose wooden chair—a seating and storage essential in a well-ordered bathroom.

RIGHT In this airy bathroom with its traditional tiled floor, an antique washstand has been converted into a modern plumbed basin unit. It looks exactly as it might have 100 years ago, save for the wall faucets and modern ceramic basin rising above the washstand. The traditional design, with its open shelves, provides space for storing towels and other necessities.

bathrooms

For centuries the washing arrangement in the French country house was a basin and ewer in the bedroom, with a portable bathtub kept either in the room or elsewhere. Perhaps on account of this, the French country bathroom has a slightly impermanent air and seems to be something of an afterthought—which, of course, in many cases, it was.

One characteristic of French bathrooms is that they seem slightly recycled. The fixtures might include, for example, a restored roll-top bathtub, basins set into what was once a marble-topped washstand for a basin and pitcher, and towels hanging over a folding towel rod. Actually, many basins are not inset at all; many new-style basins look like bowls and appear to rest artfully on the surface, just like the china bowls of the 19th century, but with efficient 21st-century plumbing concealed below.

Old washstands, with or without inset basins, are almost universally used; many have marble tops, but sometimes the surface is wood. Whether they have a cupboard beneath or open shelves, the base is given over to practical purposes and used for the storage of towels and linen.

The manner in which these old washstands are recycled illustrates the refreshing attitude of French people toward antique furniture in the bathroom. They like it, and they have perfected the art of utilizing pieces that seem—even if it is not in fact the case—to have been designed for other rooms and other purposes, but which work very well in their new setting. Take the case of mirrors, for example. There is no nonsense about mirrors being easy to clean and condensation-free; bathroom mirrors in the French countryside are whatever works best

decoratively speaking and may well be oversized and heavily gilded if that is what gives the right effect. "Integral lighting" and "built-in" are phrases that are not often heard. Pictures also are picked for effect rather than anti-steam durability. The bathroom is as important a room as any other and should have pretty things on the walls, regardless of what medium or frame they are in.

As seen in the case of the freestanding basins, French country style decrees that, even though some of the furniture might be old, there is no need for the core services to be old-fashioned. French plumbing might once have been the subject of vaudeville jokes, but these days it is as technically advanced as anywhere else in the world. There is not, it is fair to say, the

same emphasis on the power of the shower—indeed, there is not always a separate shower in a bathroom at all. A note on bath/shower curtains: instead of having a plastic shower curtain on view to the world, French country bathrooms often have an inner waterproof lining, hidden by another, strictly unwaterproof curtain that hangs outside the bathtub and might be made from voile or lightweight cotton.

So, notwithstanding the effectiveness of the power shower, most ablutions in the French country bathroom take place around the bathtub, basin, and, of course, the bidet—that essentially French piece of equipment whose usefulness is not appreciated by people in many other countries; yet, like a solid-fuel range, once used, a bidet is rarely relinquished.

BELOW LEFT In keeping with the elemental design of this house in the Luberon, the bathroom is en suite in the finest sense—in that it is separated from the bedroom by no more than a low stone wall, which hides all the practical elements from sight, while making possible instant access.

BELOW A solid wood washstand demands some color on the walls in this bathroom—here, a pale Tiffany blue color is used, set off by white-painted relief molding. The body of the roll-top freestanding bathtub is painted the same soft pale blue as the walls, and the floor is made of warm terra-cotta tiles.

OPPOSITE, LEFT A converted washstand, made into a double unit, stands in the corner of a light bathroom. The fact that there is plenty of surface space—enough even for a glass vase of spring flowers, not to mention space for towel storage under the basins—makes this an immensely useful piece. Add a simple white curtain and unadorned mirrors, and you have the perfect country bathroom.

OPPOSITE, RIGHT A freestanding roll-top bathtub is paired with a ladder-style freestanding towel rod and a crystal-drop chandelier. White walls, a stool with extra towels, and a comfortable rug complete the picture.

OPPOSITE **Julie Prisca's bathroom in her Normandy farmhouse is an unconventional take on a traditional idea. The basin is set into a freestanding unit that stands in the center of the room on a wrought-iron base; it is complete with wall lights and storage below for towels and bathroom essentials. Following tradition, the bathtub stands beneath the window to take advantage of the natural light.**

Plumbing aside, the one thing that French country bathrooms do not do is to fall into the specially designed products trap—not for the French the grotesquely obvious theme-park bathrooms. There are no opaque shower curtains decorated with grinning goldfish or bath tiles sporting a design of watery reeds and sodden ducks; each element is taken at its aesthetic worth, rather than for its attention-grabbing value. And towels are always predominantly white—sometimes with the addition of a single band of pale color or a woven self-colored design.

But it is far from dull. There is color there, but it is subtle and understated. A French country bathroom keeps its welcome muted, preferring pale plaster color or colors that recall the freshness of water and daylight; primary colors are not wanted. There is pattern—but it is rarely from paper or fabric, coming instead from the traditional motifs, usually geometric and monochromatic, on wall tiles.

The tiles that are used on bathroom walls are often made locally; tilemaking is considered a great art in many parts of

ABOVE LEFT **This pared-down country house has a connecting bathroom with a difference. Instead of a door leading into the bathroom space, it has been enclosed by a simple wooden shutter, painted black, which hides the everyday workings of basin and bathtub.**

ABOVE **In this interpretation of an old washstand brought up to date, the wooden top has had a modern basin set into it, with a single, rather traditional spout fitted to one side of the basin and two faucets on the other. An oval wrought-iron mirror completes the picture.**

BELOW A French country bathroom does not have to be decorated in neutral shades. Color works well, too, as shown in this room dominated by an antique wooden washstand. To match the strength of the furniture, the walls have been painted terra-cotta pink, which provides a subtle background for the gilded mirror as well as the washstand. The diaphanous window curtain gives the room a subtle diffused light.

RIGHT The ocher-washed walls in this bathroom act as a dramatic foil for the gold-framed antique cartouches, as well as for the linen curtained, marble-topped washstand.

RIGHT A simple period washstand has been cleverly modernized; as so often in French country style, an inset sink has been substituted for the original freestanding bowl, embellished by a traditional folding towel rod. The balance between contemporary and traditional is nicely observed.

OPPOSITE This is an example of a connecting bathroom laid out in the grand manner: a traditional roll-top cast-iron tub that has been painted to match the room is backed by an arresting group of tiles and made even more dramatic by a mirror worthy of the most imposing of rooms.

The slightly make-do-and-mend air can be charming. Why spend the entire decorating budget on the bathroom when there are so many more interesting things to do in the house with the money?

France, and the French have perfected the art of subtle handmade tiles, patterned and glazed with thin washes of color, beneath which the terra-cotta base can palely be seen.

A country bathroom is treated like a room rather than a temple to hygiene; it may have vases of flowers, and curtains—usually lightweight and very possibly unlined, they will be chosen, like everything else in the room, for their charm rather than their practical merits. On the floor, too, tiles are generally laid—either waxed and sealed terra cotta or glazed and patterned ceramic tiles. Unlike in some bathrooms, wall-to-wall carpet is not seen—but almost anywhere in a French country house, it would be a contradiction in style terms.

The connecting, or ensuite, bathroom so keenly sought in other countries—ironically, named from a French phrase that has been happily adopted by the English-speaking world—is not always considered to be the most desirable of layouts. Of course, the bathroom may indeed lead off the bedroom into a separate room, or even be in the bedroom itself, but equally it may, in an old house, be carved out of a particularly thick wall, or possibly be situated in another part of the house altogether. Sometimes, in properties where there are buildings to spare, the bathroom may even be outside the house—in an old dairy or stable, for example. Wherever it is, there will be a feeling of light freshness that makes it a room in which to linger.

LEFT **Wooden walls, a simple wooden washstand, a hidden chair, and a circular table in the window make this a room to be enjoyed.**

ABOVE **An old basin has had a curtain gathered around it, making** an area for storage. **The whole area is decorated more as a corner of a bedroom than a bathroom.**

RIGHT **The gilded bed canopy over the tub in this grand room dates from the time of Louis XIV.**

Over the centuries, the hall has gradually changed from being, in its earliest inception, the busy social heart of the house to later becoming an anteroom, a place where servants and visitors waited to be seen. In cities and towns over the years, the hall became progressively smaller, culminating in nothing more than a glorified corridor. In the countryside however, the hall remained large—often more of a reception room than a waiting room—a room that was an appropriate setting for the often imposing central flight of stairs. And nowhere is this more clearly felt than in the hall of a French country house, which often seems to be as interesting a room as the others leading from it.

The nature of the floor is central to a French country hall. Obviously, it will be made of a practical material. It may be stone, it may even be cobbled; it may be tiled, either in a striking pattern—black and white squares are the traditional choice, or sometimes handmade terra-cotta tiles; polished wood is another option, but whatever it is, it is always allowed to show off its beauty on its own. The hall of a French country house would never

ABOVE **When is a hall is not a hall? When it is floored in the same finish as the courtyard beyond. The cobbles inside are as strong as, if not stronger than, they would be outside. It is interesting to see the successful contrast between tough floor and delicate table.**

OPPOSITE **The same interior design scheme is seen here in its entirety—it is obvious how large a part the curved staircase plays within the final scheme. Note the use of a traditional French curved-back settee, as well as an antique console table.**

hallways & other spaces

In a country house, whether French, British, or American, the hall has many roles. On both practical and aesthetic levels, it is a transitional space between the street and the house, and the house and yard. It is also, or should be, a welcoming space—the first, important impression that a guest has of the house beyond. Last but not least, the hall can be a useful repository for many of the essentials of indoor–outdoor life.

OPPOSITE The oversized always works within a classically arranged setting that gives due consideration to scale and harmony. This hall, with its gracious stairs, leads majestically to the open air; the oversized urn merely emphasizes the decorative simplicity.

LEFT Simple is as simple does: this whole area is designed to look understated. The walls are decorated in a particular specialist finish involving traditional limewash, which gives an old, almost static, feeling to the whole scheme.

BELOW It is clever to have an important focal point at the base of a staircase to which the eye can be drawn. Here, a freestanding bookcase plays an important role in the arrangement of objects and furniture.

have a carpeted floor—what would be the point of that? (Although it might have an old flat-weave rug, or rush or sisal matting spread over it.)

A French country hall is never treated as a repository for furniture that doesn't fit in anywhere else. Here there are objects and furniture, always few in number, that demand to be looked at— swagger pieces essentially. There is always a striking table, for example, often one of some distinction such as an antique console table, and every country hall worthy of its name should have a mirror— essential for first and last glimpses—which should be large enough to reflect light as well as features, and decorative enough to be worth looking at. There should also be some form of seating: a bench at the very least, or a pair of chairs or even a small upright banquette.

Generally wallpaper is not used in a hall, being considered more suitable for private rooms such as the bedroom. The paint colors used in a French country hall are based on much the same principle as the colors used in the rest of the house; they will be light, reflective, and gentle—soft creams perhaps and pale grays, combined with contrasting woodwork, with large areas, such as the door, painted in several tones of one color. What they will not be is cold, glossy, or harsh.

A common decorating mistake in a square hall with a central staircase is to choose too small a central light. If the staircase is particularly commanding, it is important that the light is large enough and striking enough not only to illuminate both the ground floor and the stairs, but also to be able to hold its own against the dominating architectural features. Many French country halls have large lanterns descending low into the stair-well that both illuminate and balance the curve of the stairs. If

RIGHT This interesting group combines a finely made open staircase, book shelves, and, most importantly, a large open fireplace. The antique armchair adds gravitas to the decorative scheme.

OPPOSITE, LEFT If you cannot incorporate enough bookcases in one room, consider a gallery, no matter how narrow, to hold the remainder. A gallery of any sort looks impressive from below as well as at eye level.

OPPOSITE, ABOVE RIGHT If your bookcase is a talking point—that is, made into a gallery—then it is important that it seems worth talking about. Here the books have been arranged not only by volume but also as objects in their own right, with each compartment offering a visual treat.

OPPOSITE, BELOW RIGHT The ironwork stairs and the balcony above make a satisfying configuration that is as pleasing to the eye above as it is below.

Paint colors will be light, reflective, and gentle—soft creams perhaps and pale grays, combined with contrasting woodwork, with large areas painted in several tones of one color.

OPPOSITE How different an 18th-century decorative scheme is from one of the 19th century. In this 19th-century example, there is a simplicity and austerity that would be absent in something from the earlier epoch. The tiles, possibly encaustic, are echoed by the subdued colorings of walls and woodwork.

LEFT In this back hall of an old manor house, as in the manner of back halls everywhere, pieces are used together that were never intended for such use. The prie-dieu, coupled with a bedroom chair and a decorative side table, make a charming set-piece, but without much decorative narrative.

BELOW This is a disciplined and harmonious grouping, with the choice of furniture being dictated by the stylish floor tile, a type of decorative tile reminiscent of colored cement provençal tiles of a century earlier.

the hall is particularly large, there are usually other sources of light—lamps and wall lights—to give warmth as well as to welcome and show the arriving guest the way forward.

The hall has always been seen as a good, almost gallerylike, space in which to display pictures. Any pictures should be large enough to hold their own within the space; in a French country house, pictures are used sparingly in the hall, as they are in other rooms, often limited to one or two within the central area.

Decorative objects, too, are always in proportion and scale with the size of the hall itself. The table might hold a bowl or vase of flowers, and there may be a large urn or pot at floor level that looks attractive on its own, but which can also double as an umbrella or walking-cane holder. But there will be little extraneous clutter, because in French country style the aim is, in every room, to achieve as airy and open a sense of space as possible.

LEFT An outside corner can be as inviting as one indoors, and decorated with as much care; this sunny spot has a small circular metal table covered with a fresh cloth, geraniums in blue-painted Versailles planters, and decorative birdcages hung around the walls.

RIGHT Once the home of Nicole de Vesian, this glorious house in the Luberon is as much about outdoors as it is about interior spaces. The garden—with its almost abstract topiary—is architectural in form while retaining a fluid living element.

Throughout rural France, both in the villages and in the more sparsely populated open countryside, a close relationship is fostered between house and garden, for there is indeed a harmonious link between the two—between the manmade and the natural world, as well as between the present and the past. Old houses, new houses, even those decorated in contemporary fashion, maintain a virtually seamless connection with that which went before, and that which surrounds them—both in the immediate environment and in the wider landscape.

A natural product of this intimate relationship between the inside and outside of the house is a domesticated outdoor space of some description. The outside living area may be a porch attached to the house, a terrace, or simply somewhere in the garden or the fields beyond—either a favorite spot under a tree or near water, or perhaps a more permanent structure such as an arbor, tent, or open-sided summerhouse, frequently quite distant from the house itself.

Naturally, the same rules are followed outside the house as would be applied in the interior. An outdoor room, however simple in style, should be practical and comfortable in all its aspects, and

outdoor rooms

Rare is the French country house that does not have a living area somewhere outside. It will have been designed as somewhere to sit and dream, read, eat, or drink, and it will be arranged and furnished as such—it is as much part of the house as any room within.

The outside living area may be no more than a favorite spot under a tree or near water, or perhaps a more permanent structure such as an arbor, tent, or open-sided summerhouse.

endowed with an air of pleasant decoration deriving from beautiful objects, comfortable chairs and the presence of flowers and plants, whether growing or cut.

Although white molded-plastic garden tables and chairs are unfortunately ubiquitous in France—and very unattractive they are, too—the exponents of French country style look in a different direction for garden furniture. For them, the watchword is natural, and the furniture they choose might be new but it could also be antique. Old metal, in the form of antique cast-iron benches and chairs, is particularly prized. Old chairs are difficult to find and usually expensive, although there are modern versions taken from the originals that look good

and last a lifetime. Many people like the quintessentially French wrought-metal table, chairs, and benches, which are not so hard to track down. Wrought metal does not have to be old, though—new versions are easily found, painted either in a green so dark as to be almost black or in pale driftwood shades.

Wooden tables and chairs are frequently not oiled, but either stained a color or left to age gently; wicker and cane chairs, both armchairs and uprights—rather reminiscent of a Proustian garden party—are often painted in grays, blues, and greens, and then allowed to weather and fade.

Cushions for all these seating arrangements are all-important in order to achieve the required level of comfort, and therefore

OPPOSITE, LEFT A pretty metal garden chair placed against the wall in the shade of an old fig tree, and offering sweeping views of the countryside, is the center of an almost perfect composition.

OPPOSITE, RIGHT A balcony at the top of an open staircase has been made into a small sunny eating area—the perfect place for taking breakfast or tea. An old-fashioned mosquito net has been draped over the table, and slatted-back chairs wait to be occupied.

ABOVE Instead of a metal or wooden table, a sturdy stone table serves as somewhere to congregate and a substantial surface for food and drink. Set beside a shady tree, and with a stone planter at its center, it becomes an almost sculptural piece.

ABOVE RIGHT A tower on the Ile de Ré boasts a quintessentially French outdoor room, with a traditional wrought-iron round table and light folding chairs. The raised beds with their lavender and geraniums in full bloom look like large vases of garden flowers.

RIGHT Tiles that were used indoors have also been put to good use outside, having been broken up and re-formed to make a charming mosaic of blue and white.

BELOW **This scene embraces some of the admirable elements of French country style: an old stone wall, unremarkable but also untouched, a pair of folded chairs, an urn ready for planting, and some exuberant foliage.**

RIGHT **True French country style finds a place for everything— nothing is wasted or discarded. Here, wire baskets hang at the ready in a barn alongside an empty picture frame; perhaps the picture is at this moment being painted?**

RIGHT **Everything in this open-sided barn is redolent of the enjoyment of the open air. Not only are there ladders and garden tools, but also urns and pitchers, chunky candles—and even a straw summer hat.**

there is always an abundance of them. In French country style, outdoor cushions give the impression that they have come out of the house a few moments earlier—which, in many cases, they have. There may be rounded seat cushions and other, less formal shapes. Of assorted sizes, they will be covered in striped and checked designs, soft flower prints, and plain linens. Designs with neon-bright colors or garden motifs will not be in evidence, however; French country style is very different from Florida country style in that respect.

Eating meals in an outdoor room demands—and is granted— as much respect as eating inside. Tablecloths and napkins are both used; the cloth will usually be large, and it will rarely be fitted. An important aspect of French country style is the understanding—probably unspoken—that everything should

look as if it had always been there, that nothing should appear specially made or purpose-built. On the table there will be fresh flowers, preferably from the garden, in pitchers or small glass vases, and the food will be served in wooden and terra-cotta dishes, and presented with as much care as it would be in the dining room or kitchen. Stackable opaque plastic boxes with close-fitting colored lids are nowhere to be seen. Plates and glasses are simple but genuine—no cheerful plastic with daisy prints, but piles of colored pottery and sturdy glasses, although for a treat the best china and glass may be transported to an outside table.

Lighting is a mixture of the practical and the decorative— where the outside space is too far distant from the house to make electric light practicable (and some people eschew that

option in any event), there may be, on the tables, candles inside bell-shaped glass hurricane lamps of different heights and sizes. Around the central area there will be small tea-lights used for the same purpose as background lighting would be in the house—to give depth and additional interest. The tea-lights might be placed in colored glass jars on the ground or suspended from stems and branches in anything from glass jars to pierced metal lanterns, perhaps combined with colored-paper Chinese lanterns.

Plant containers are important outside the house, having as they do both practical and decorative roles. It probably goes without saying that no flowerpot-colored plastic pots will be discovered in the French country garden. Exponents of French country style have always valued their old hand-

thrown terra-cotta flowerpots and buy them whenever they see them, using them both as cachepots and as functional plant-growing vessels. Other containers may be made of stone in the form of urns or jars, and if there are wooden containers, they will either be the straight-sided containers known as Versailles pots or curved tub shapes.

The design of the garden itself will be painted with the same brush as the interior of the house. It will not have a regimented layout nor will it be self-consciously pretty—but it will be relaxed and relatively easy to maintain. Grass commonly plays a large part in the French country garden—traditionally, the tall windows that we call French doors were constructed to open directly onto lawn without the interruption of flowerbeds, a device that reinforces the connection between inside and out.

OPPOSITE Made for relaxation, with its chairs, benches, and masses of pillows, this sunny seating area, surrounded by trees and shrubs in very large pots, shows how a small space can be made both inviting and welcoming.

ABOVE This space is half potting shed, half conservatory, as well as being a pleasant place to sit and dream—or work. A canvas stool and plants in bloom, as well as in every stage of growth, make it an ideal retreat.

ABOVE RIGHT Proof that all is not quite as it seems in what is ostensibly an area for work: a telltale cup of coffee and an open book testify to the therapeutic qualities of the space.

RIGHT In the garden created by Nicole de Vesian, the tables and chairs seem to be almost part of the plantlife surrounding them.

ABOVE Roses climbing up a rough plaster wall, a cluster of pink geraniums, and a courtyard laid with stones on which are placed an inviting pair of chairs and a table: this is French country style at its most natural.

ABOVE RIGHT An old lantern suspended from a wooden peg in a stone wall is the centerpiece of a scene that could have been put together yesterday or 200 years ago.

RIGHT These metal racks designed for plant containers are traditional in shape and color and are made today in the same way they were a century ago. The curls and flounces of the ironwork beautifully set off the recently harvested tomatoes.

OPPOSITE, ABOVE LEFT Any sheltered area, from a formal courtyard to a working farmyard, can be given a little charm as long as the vital ingredients for comfort and pleasure are there.

OPPOSITE, ABOVE RIGHT A set of wooden shelves provides an ideal surface for holding the food and drink prepared for an alfresco meal.

OPPOSITE, BELOW LEFT This chic palanquin has been designed for one thing only—to create a comfortable, even luxurious space for outdoor living, complete with snow-white day beds.

OPPOSITE, BELOW RIGHT Even the simplest garden bench can be made inviting if it is furnished with a pretty pillow and throw.

There is an understanding that everything should look as if it had always been there, that nothing should appear specially made.

resources

FABRICS

C.M OFFRAY & SONS, INC.
Route 24, P.O. Box 601
Chester, NJ 07930
(908)-879-4700
Fabric, notions, and trims from retailers nationwide.

FINE ARTS BUILDING
232 East Ninth Street
New York, NY 10022
(212)-223-0373
Aged and faded florals, many based on an archive of antique French fabrics.

FRETTE
799 Madison Avenue
New York, NY 10021
(212)-988-5221
Elegant linens, including French imports.

LA PROVENCE
239 Chartres Street
New Orleans, LA 70130
(504)-299-0772
www.provencelinens.com
Linens from the South of France.

PETER FASANO, LTD.
964 South Main Street
Great Barrington, MA 01230
(413)-528-6872
Antique and contemporary textiles.

PIERRE DEUX
879 Madison Avenue
New York, NY 10021
www.pierredeux.com
(212)-570-9343
French country wallpaper, fabric, upholstery, and antiques.

PIERRE FREY, INC.
12 East 33rd Street
New York, NY 10019
(212)-213-3099
Fabrics and wall coverings, including printed cottons based on an archive of 18th- and 19th-century French fabrics.

SALAMANDRE SILK, INC.
950 Third Avenue
New York, NY 10022
(718)-361-8500
Restores classic fabrics for historic houses and sells trims, wallpaper, textiles, and custom carpets.

THIBAUT
480 Frelinghuysen Avenue
Newark, NJ 07114
(800)-223-0704
Textile dealer specializing in wallpaper.

YVES DELORME
1725 Broadway
Charlottesville, CA 22902
To find a retailer near you, visit
www.yvesdelorme.com
(800)-322-3911
Sophisticated French bed linens.

FLOORING

ANN SACKS TILE & STONE
8120 NE 33rd Drive
Portland, OR 97211
(800)-969-5217
www.annsacks.com
High-quality tiles and stone surfaces.

COUNTRY FLOORS
15 East 16th Street
New York, NY 10003
(212)-627-8300
www.countryfloors.com
Country-style ceramics and terra cotta.

PARIS CERAMICS
151 Greenwich Avenue
Greenwich, CT 06830
(203)-552-9658
www.parisceramics.com
Limestone, terra cotta, antique stone, and hand-painted tiles.

STONE PANELS
1725 Sandy Lake Road
Carrollton, TX 75006
(972)-446-1776 or (800)-328-6275
www.stonepanels.com
Stone surfaces, from limestone to granite to marble.

WALKER ZANGER
8901 Bradley Avenue
Sun Valley, CA 91352
(818)-504-0235
www.walkerzanger.com
Tiles in every material, including metal, terra cotta, and glass.

FURNITURE

BREMERMANN DESIGNS
3943 Magazine Street
New Orleans, LA 70015
www.neworleansantiquesdealers.com
(504)-891-7763
French antiques and accessories imported from Europe.

BRIMFIELD ANTIQUE SHOW
Route 20, Brimfield, MA 01010
(413)-245-3436
www.brimfieldshow.com
This famous flea market, which features dealers are from all over the U.S. and from Europe, runs for a week in May, July, and September. For listings of other flea markets around the country, visit www.fleamarket.com.

CHARLES P. ROGERS
55 West 17th Street
New York, NY 10011
(212)-675-4400
www.charlesprogers.com
Brass and iron beds; European linens.

CHÂTEAU DOMINGUE
3615-B West Alabama Street
Houston, TX 77027
(713)-961-3444
www.ChateauDominque.com
Antique furniture and accessories.

CISAR HOLT
1609 East 15th Street
Tulsa, OK 74120
(918)-582-3080
Reproduction French furniture.

COUNTRY FRENCH INTERIORS
1428 Slocum Street
Dallas, TX 75207
(214)-747-4700
www.countryfrenchinteriors.com
French country-style antiques.

THE FARMHOUSE COLLECTION, INC.
P.O. Box 3089
Twin Falls, ID 83303
(208)-736-8700
Rustic furniture, including French style.

THE FRENCH ATTIC
116 Bennett Street
Atlanta, GA 30309
(404)-352-4430
www.thestalls.com
An eclectic selection of antiques.

FRENCH COUNTRY ANTIQUES
100 King Street
Alexandria, VA 22314
(703)-548-8563
The name says it all.

HOWARD KAPLAN ANTIQUES
827 Broadway
New York, NY 10003
(212)-674-1000
www.howardkaplanantiques.com
French antiques and reproductions.

JANE KELTNER
136 Cumberland Boulevard
Memphis, TN 38112
(901)-458-7476
www.janekeltner.com
Painted furniture.

LYMAN DRAKE ANTIQUES
2901 South Harbor Boulevard
Santa Ana, CA 92704
(714)-979-2811
Antique French furnishings.

MAISON FELICE
73-960 El Paso Drive
Palm Desert, CA 92260
(760)-862-0021
www.maisonfelice.com
European antiques and furnishings.

OLD TIMBER TABLE COMPANY
908 Dragon Street
Dallas, TX 75207
(214)-761-1882
Country-style tables.

SAM SPACEK
8212 East 41st Street
Tulsa, OK 74145
(918)-627-3021
French antiques.

THERIEN AND COMPANY
716 North La Cienega Boulevard
Los Angeles, CA 90069
(310)-657-4615
www.therien.com
Period antique furniture.

GARDEN FURNITURE AND ORNAMENTS

ARCHIPED CLASSICS
315 Cole Street
Dallas, TX 75207
(214)-748-7437
www.archipedclassics.com
Classic garden ornaments.

BARBARA ISRAEL GARDEN ANTIQUES
296 Mount Holly Road
Katonah, NY 10536
(212)-744-6286
www.bi-gardenantiques.com
By appointment only.

ELIZABETH STREET GARDEN AND GALLERY
1176 Second Avenue
New York, NY 10021
(212)-644-6969
www.elizabethstreetgallery.com
Antiques and reproductions.

PAINTS

OLD FASHIONED MILK PAINT CO.
436 Main Street, P.O. Box 222
Groton, MA 01450
(478)-448-6336
www.milkpaint.com
Paints made from natural pigments.

**PRATT AND LAMBERT
HISTORIC PAINTS**
To find a retail outlet near you, visit
www.prattandlambert.com
Top-of-the-line paints.

STULB'S OLD VILLAGE PAINT
P.O. Box 1030
Fort WA, PA 19034
(215)-654-1770
Vintage colors for furniture and walls.

ACCESSORIES

ANTHROPOLOGIE
1700 Sansom Street, 6th floor
Philadelphia, PA 19103
For stores, call (800)-309-2500 or visit
www.anthropologie.com.
Vintage-inspired home accessories

THE ANTIQUE HARDWARE STORE
19 Buckingham Plantation Drive
Bluffon, SC 29910
(800)-422-9982
Unusual and antique hardware.

FRENCH COUNTRY LIVING
10205 Calvin Run Road
Great Falls, VA 22066
(800)-485-1302
French country–style accessories.

HOULÈS USA, INC.
8594 Melrose Avenue
Los Angleles, CA 90069
(310)-652-6171
www.houles.com
*Fine trimmings and passementerie
from this French retailer.*

LA MAISON MODERNE
144 West 19th Street
New York, NY 10011
(212)-691-9603
French accessories.

LE POTAGER
108 West Brookdale Place
Fullerton, CA 92832
(714)-680-8864
Trimmings and decorative details.

P. E. GUERIN, INC.
21 to 23 Jane Street
New York, NY 10014
(212)-243-5270
www.peguerin.com
Decorative hardware.

ROMANCING PROVENCE, LTD.
225 Fifth Avenue
New York, Ny 10010
(212)-481-9879
French country imports.

RENAISSANCE RIBBONS
P.O. Box 699
Oregon House, CA 95961
(530)-692-0842
www.renaissanceribbons.com
Trimmings and notions.

business credits
*designers and establishments
featured in this book*

**ANNIE-CAMILLE KUENTZMANN-
LEVET DÉCORATION**
3 Ter, Rue Mathieu Le Coz
La Noue, 78980 Mondreville
France
+ 33-1-30-42-53-59
Pages 9, 15l, 18, 34, 35a, 43l, 44b,
49, 57, 62al, 71r, 79, 89r, 108r, 121,
130, 137a.

ARNE TENGBLAD Artist
+ 33-4-90-72-38-44
Arteng@wanadoo.fr
Pages 4cl, 52bl, 53r, 56, 90l, 96b,
106, 107l, 109, 132l, 134l, 138ar.

LA BASTIDE DE MARIE
Route de Bonnieux
84560 Ménerbes
France
+ 33-4-90-72-30-20
www.c-h-m.com
Pages 24, 40a, 61, 67a, 86, 96a,
103b, 125b, 126, 138br.

CAROLE OULHEN
Interior Designer
tel + 33-6-80-99-66-16
fax + 33-4-90-02-01 91
With the help of contractors:
Icardi Soditra Entreprise
+ 33-4-90-89-31-52
Pages 6, 19b, 36, 44a, 47r, 59r, 62bl,
67c, 71l, 92–93, 113, 114r, 128.

CHATEAU DE GIGNAC
Gignac en Provence 84400
France
+ 33-4-90-04-84-33
Pages 13, 22l, 23, 42r, 53bl, 67b,
68–69, 76–77, 102, 115r, 118–119,
122–123, 136.

DAISY SIMON
Architecte D'Interieur Décoration
55 Cours Mirabeau
Passage Agard
13100 Aix-en-Provence
France
daisy.simonaix@wanadoo.fr
Pages 19a, 37, 39b, 46, 74–75,
98, 103a, 114l.

DOMAINE DE LA BARONNIE
21 Rue Baron de Chantal
17410 St-Martin de Ré
France
+ 33-5-46-09-21 29
www.domainedelabaronnie.com
Pages 16b, 71cl, 72–73, 110–111l,
133, 138al.

FRENCH COUNTRY LIVING
Antiques & Decoration
21 Rue De L'Eglise
06250 Mougins
France
+ 33-4-93-75-53-03
f.c.l.com@wanadoo.fr
Pages 4cr & r, 16a, 41, 43r, 45, 47l,
52a & br, 62br, 88, 89l, 105, 111r.

IPL INTERIORS
25 Bullen Street
Battersea
London SW11 3ER
UK
+ 44-(0)20-7978-4224
Also involved in this project:
Pierre-Marie Gilles, Paris
+ 33-1-46-04-82-49
Pages 11cl, 20a, 25–27, 30–31,
60, 64–65, 104a, 107r, 115l, 127,
131, 137b.

ISABELLE SCHOUTEN
Collection Privée Antiquités
www.collection-privee.com
Pages 1, 3, 5, 11l, 42l, 50, 62ar, 66,
70, 82–83, 97, 100–101, 124, 125a.

J&M DAVIDSON
Gallery:
97 Golborne Road
London W10 5NL
UK
Shop:
42 Ledbury Road
London W11 2SE
UK
Pages 54l, 55, 80–81, 85, 112, 129a.

JEAN-GABRIEL LALOY
Interior Designer
Les Fusains—La Rue
50440 Vauville
France
Pages 4l, 20b, 28–29, 32–33, 35b,
48, 87, 104b, 120.

JULIE PRISCA
46 Rue du Bac
75007 Paris
France
+ 33-1-45-48-13-29
infos@julieprisca.com
www.julieprisca.com
Pages 22r, 39a, 95, 116, 134r, 135,
139bl.

LINUM
+ 33-4-90-38-37-38
www.linum-france.com
linum@dial.oleane.com
Pages 4cl, 52bl, 53r, 56, 90l, 96b,
106, 107l, 109, 132l, 134l, 138ar.

LA MAISON DOUCE
25 rue Mérindot
17410 St-Martin de Ré
France
+ 33-5-46-09-20-20
www.lamaisondouce.com
Pages 14, 15r, 71cr, 99, 108l,
117, 132r.

**MIREILLE AND JEAN CLAUDE
LOTHON**
La Cour Beaudeval Antiquities
4 rue des Fontaines
28210 Faverolles
France
+ 33-2-37-51-47-67
Pages 2, 10, 11cr & r, 12, 17, 38, 40b,
51, 53al, 54r, 58, 59l, 63, 78, 84, 90r,
91, 94, 129b, 139a & br.

picture credits

Photography by Christopher Drake unless otherwise stated.

Key: a=above, b=below, r=right, l=left, c=center.

1 A country house near Mougins, Provence; 2 Owners of La Cour Beaudeval Antiquities, Mireille and Jean Claude Lothon's house in Faverolles; 3 A country house near Mougins, Provence; 4l A Normandy manor house restored by interior designer Jean-Gabriel Laloy; 4cl Anna Bonde and artist Arne Tengblad's home in the Luberon Valley, Provence; 4cr & r Owners of French Country Living, the Hill family's home on the Cote D'Azur; 5 A country house near Mougins, Provence; 6 Interior designer Carole Oulhen; 9 Annie-Camille Kuentzmann-Levet's house in the Yvelines; 10 Owners of La Cour Beaudeval Antiquities, Mireille and Jean Claude Lothon's house in Faverolles; 11l A country house near Mougins, Provence; 11cl A country house in the Luberon, Provence with interior design by François Gilles and Dominque Lubar of IPL Interiors and Pierre-Marie Gilles, Paris; 11cr, r & 12 Owners of La Cour Beaudeval Antiquities, Mireille and Jean Claude Lothon's house in Faverolles; 13 The Chateau de Gignac, Michelle Joubert's home in Provence; 14 Alain et Catherine Brunel's home and hotel, La Maison Douce, St-Martin de Ré; 15l Annie-Camille Kuentzmann-Levet's house in the Yvelines; 15r Alain et Catherine Brunel's home and hotel, La Maison Douce, St-Martin de Ré; 16a Owners of French Country Living, the Hill family's home on the Cote D'Azur; 16b Florence and Pierre Pallardy, Domaine de la Baronnie, St-Martin de Ré; 17 Owners of La Cour Beaudeval Antiquities, Mireille and Jean Claude Lothon's house in Faverolles; 18 Annie-Camille Kuentzmann-Levet's house in the Yvelines; 19a A family home near Aix-en-Provence with interior design by Daisy Simon; 19b Interior designer Carole Oulhen; 20a A country house in the Luberon, Provence with interior design by François Gilles and Dominque Lubar of IPL Interiors and Pierre-Marie Gilles, Paris; 20b & 21 A Normandy manor house restored by interior designer Jean-Gabriel Laloy; 22l The Chateau de Gignac, Michelle Joubert's home in Provence; 22r Julie Prisca's house in Normandy; 23 The Chateau de Gignac, Michelle Joubert's home in Provence; 24 La Bastide de Marie, Ménerbes; 25-27 A country house in the Luberon, Provence with interior design by François Gilles and Dominque Lubar of IPL Interiors and Pierre-Marie Gilles, Paris; 28–29 A Normandy manor house restored by interior designer Jean-Gabriel Laloy; 30–31 A country house in the Luberon, Provence with interior design by François Gilles and Dominque Lubar of IPL Interiors and Pierre-Marie Gilles, Paris; 32–33 A Normandy manor house restored by interior designer Jean-Gabriel Laloy; 34 & 35a Annie-Camille Kuentzmann-Levet's house in the Yvelines; 35b A Normandy manor house restored by interior designer Jean-Gabriel Laloy; 36 Interior designer Carole Oulhen; 37 A family home near Aix-en-Provence with interior design by Daisy Simon; 38 Owners of La Cour Beaudeval Antiquities, Mireille and Jean Claude Lothon's house in Faverolles; 39a Julie Prisca's house in Normandy; 39b A family home near Aix-en-Provence with interior design by Daisy Simon; 40a La Bastide de Marie, Ménerbes; 40b Owners of La Cour Beaudeval Antiquities, Mireille and Jean Claude Lothon's house in Faverolles; 41 Owners of French Country Living, the Hill family's home on the Cote D'Azur; 42l A country house near Mougins, Provence; 42r The Chateau de Gignac, Michelle Joubert's home in Provence; 43l Annie-Camille Kuentzmann-Levet's house in the Yvelines; 43r Owners of French Country Living, the Hill family's home on the Cote D'Azur; 44a Interior designer Carole Oulhen; 44b Annie-Camille Kuentzmann-Levet's house in the Yvelines; 45 Owners of French Country Living, the Hill family's home on the Cote D'Azur; 46 A family home near Aix-en-Provence with interior design by Daisy Simon; 47l Owners of French Country Living, the Hill family's home on the Cote D'Azur; 47r Interior designer Carole Oulhen; 48 A Normandy manor house restored by interior designer Jean-Gabriel Laloy; 49 Annie-Camille Kuentzmann-Levet's house in the Yvelines; 50 A country house near Mougins, Provence; 51 Owners of La Cour Beaudeval Antiquities, Mireille and Jean Claude Lothon's house in Faverolles; 52a & br Owners of French Country Living, the Hill family's home on the Cote D'Azur; 52bl & 53r Anna Bonde and artist Arne Tengblad's home in the Luberon Valley, Provence; 53al Owners of La Cour Beaudeval Antiquities, Mireille and Jean Claude Lothon's house in Faverolles; 53bl The Chateau de Gignac, Michelle Joubert's home in Provence; 54l Owner Monique Davidson's family home in Normandy; 54r Owners of La Cour Beaudeval Antiquities, Mireille and Jean Claude Lothon's house in Faverolles; 55 Owner Monique Davidson's family home in Normandy; 56 Anna Bonde and artist Arne Tengblad's home in the Luberon Valley, Provence; 57 Annie-Camille Kuentzmann-Levet's house in the Yvelines; 58 & 59l Owners of La Cour Beaudeval Antiquities, Mireille and Jean Claude Lothon's house in Faverolles; 59r Interior designer Carole Oulhen; 60 A country house in the Luberon, Provence with interior design by François Gilles and Dominque Lubar of IPL Interiors and Pierre-Marie Gilles, Paris; 61 La Bastide de Marie, Ménerbes; 62al Annie-Camille Kuentzmann-Levet's house in the Yvelines; 62ar A country house near Mougins, Provence; 62bl Interior designer Carole Oulhen; 62br Owners of French Country Living, the Hill family's home on the Cote D'Azur; 63 Owners of La Cour Beaudeval Antiquities, Mireille and Jean Claude Lothon's house in Faverolles; 64–65 A country house in the Luberon, Provence with interior design by François Gilles and Dominque Lubar of IPL Interiors and Pierre-Marie Gilles, Paris; 66 A country house near Mougins, Provence; 67a La Bastide de Marie, Ménerbes; 67c Interior designer Carole Oulhen; 67b The Chateau de Gignac, Michelle Joubert's home in Provence; 68–69 The Chateau de Gignac, Michelle Joubert's home in Provence; 70 A country house near Mougins, Provence; 71l Interior designer Carole Oulhen; 71cl

Florence and Pierre Pallardy, Domaine de la Baronnie, St-Martin de Ré; 71cr Alain et Catherine Brunel's home and hotel, La Maison Douce, St-Martin de Ré; 71r Annie-Camille Kuentzmann-Levet's house in the Yvelines; 72–73 Florence and Pierre Pallardy, Domaine de la Baronnie, St-Martin de Ré; 74–75 A family home near Aix-en-Provence with interior design by Daisy Simon; 76–77 The Chateau de Gignac, Michelle Joubert's home in Provence; 78 Owners of La Cour Beaudeval Antiquities, Mireille and Jean Claude Lothon's house in Faverolles; 79 Annie-Camille Kuentzmann-Levet's house in the Yvelines; 80–81 Owner Monique Davidson's family home in Normandy; 82–83 A country house near Mougins, Provence; 84 Owners of La Cour Beaudeval Antiquities, Mireille and Jean Claude Lothon's house in Faverolles; 85 Owner Monique Davidson's family home in Normandy; 86 La Bastide de Marie, Ménerbes; 87 A Normandy manor house restored by interior designer Jean-Gabriel Laloy; 88 & 89l Owners of French Country Living, the Hill family's home on the Cote D'Azur; 89r Annie-Camille Kuentzmann-Levet's house in the Yvelines; 90l Anna Bonde and artist Arne Tengblad's home in the Luberon Valley, Provence; 90r & 91 Owners of La Cour Beaudeval Antiquities, Mireille and Jean Claude Lothon's house in Faverolles; 92–93 Interior designer Carole Oulhen; 94 Owners of La Cour Beaudeval Antiquities, Mireille and Jean Claude Lothon's house in Faverolles; 95 Julie Prisca's house in Normandy; 96a La Bastide de Marie, Ménerbes; 96b Anna Bonde and artist Arne Tengblad's home in the Luberon Valley, Provence; 97 A country house near Mougins, Provence; 98 A family home near Aix-en-Provence with interior design by Daisy Simon; 99 Alain et Catherine Brunel's home and hotel, La Maison Douce, St-Martin de Ré; 100–101 A country house near Mougins, Provence; 102 The Chateau de Gignac, Michelle Joubert's home in Provence; 103a A family home near Aix-en-Provence with interior design by Daisy Simon; 103b La Bastide de Marie, Ménerbes; 104a A country house in the Luberon, Provence with interior design by François Gilles and Dominque Lubar of IPL Interiors and Pierre-Marie Gilles, Paris; 104b A Normandy manor house restored by interior designer Jean-Gabriel Laloy; 105 Owners of French Country Living, the Hill family's home on the Cote D'Azur; 106 & 107l Anna Bonde and artist Arne Tengblad's home in the Luberon Valley, Provence; 107r A country house in the Luberon, Provence with interior design by François Gilles and Dominque Lubar of IPL Interiors and Pierre-Marie Gilles, Paris; 108l Alain et Catherine Brunel's home and hotel, La Maison Douce, St-Martin de Ré; 108r Annie-Camille Kuentzmann-Levet's house in the Yvelines; 109 Anna Bonde and artist Arne Tengblad's home in the Luberon Valley, Provence; 110–111l Florence and Pierre Pallardy, Domaine de la Baronnie, St-Martin de Ré; 111r Owners of French Country Living, the Hill family's home on the Cote D'Azur; 112 Owner Monique Davidson's family home in Normandy; 113 Interior designer Carole Oulhen; 114l A family home near Aix-en-Provence with interior design by Daisy Simon; 114r Interior designer Carole Oulhen; 115l A country house in the Luberon, Provence with interior design by François Gilles and Dominque Lubar of IPL Interiors and Pierre-Marie Gilles, Paris; 115r The Chateau de Gignac, Michelle Joubert's home in Provence; 116 Julie Prisca's house in Normandy; 117 Alain et Catherine Brunel's home and hotel, La Maison Douce, St-Martin de Ré; 118–119 The Chateau de Gignac, Michelle Joubert's home in Provence; 120 A Normandy manor house restored by interior designer Jean-Gabriel Laloy; 121 Annie-Camille Kuentzmann-Levet's house in the Yvelines; 122–123 The Chateau de Gignac, Michelle Joubert's home in Provence; 124 & 125a A country house near Mougins, Provence; 125b & 126 La Bastide de Marie, Ménerbes; 127 A country house in the Luberon, Provence with interior design by François Gilles and Dominque Lubar of IPL Interiors and Pierre-Marie Gilles, Paris; 128 Interior designer Carole Oulhen; 129a Owner Monique Davidson's family home in Normandy; 129b Owners of La Cour Beaudeval Antiquities, Mireille and Jean Claude Lothon's house in Faverolles; 130 Annie-Camille Kuentzmann-Levet's house in the Yvelines; 131 A country house in the Luberon, Provence with interior design by François Gilles and Dominque Lubar of IPL Interiors and Pierre-Marie Gilles, Paris; 132l Anna Bonde and artist Arne Tengblad's home in the Luberon Valley, Provence; 132r Alain et Catherine Brunel's home and hotel, La Maison Douce, St-Martin de Ré; 133 Florence and Pierre Pallardy, Domaine de la Baronnie, St-Martin de Ré; 134l Anna Bonde and artist Arne Tengblad's home in the Luberon Valley, Provence; 134r & 135 Julie Prisca's house in Normandy; 136 The Chateau de Gignac, Michelle Joubert's home in Provence; 137a Annie-Camille Kuentzmann-Levet's house in the Yvelines; 137b A country house in the Luberon, Provence with interior design by François Gilles and Dominque Lubar of IPL Interiors and Pierre-Marie Gilles, Paris; 138al Florence and Pierre Pallardy, Domaine de la Baronnie, St-Martin de Ré; 138ar Anna Bonde and artist Arne Tengblad's home in the Luberon Valley, Provence; 138br La Bastide de Marie, Ménerbes; 139a & br Owners of La Cour Beaudeval Antiquities, Mireille and Jean Claude Lothon's house in Faverolles; 139bl Julie Prisca's house in Normandy.

acknowledgments

The publishers would like to thank all those people who allowed us to photograph their beautiful homes for this book and who made us so welcome. Many thanks also to Laurent Bayard, François Gilles of IPL Interiors, and Annie-Camille Kuentzmann-Levet for their help with research.

index

Numbers in *italic* refer to captions.